His passion for acting—

He's already made forty-three movies, and won't be stopping anytime soon. He's gone from classical stage actor to bad boy of Pedro Almodovar's wacky Spanish films to Hollywood's hottest leading man. But is it art or ambition that keeps driving him forward?

His passion for music—

He built a recording studio at his villa in Madrid so he could hide out alone with his guitar... but now he's singing alongside Madonna in *Evita*. Is music the quiet secret of Antonio's strength or is he just waiting to blow us away with a voice as sexy as the rest of him?

His passion for his native land—

His soul broods for the sensuality of Spain... but when his family and country snubbed Melanie, he turned his back on them. Find out how, despite his torment, Antonio played hardball until he could have his country and his woman.

His passion for Melanie—

He went wild for her when he saw her on the screen in *Working Girl* and melted when they met at the Academy Awards. When they finally played lovers in *Two Much*, the combustion destroyed his marriage and exploded into headlines around the world.

ANTONIO BANDERAS

KATHLEEN TRACY

St. Martin's Paperbacks

ANTONIO BANDERAS

Copyright © 1996 by Kathleen Tracy.

Cover photograph by Photofest.

ISBN: 0-312-96055-7

Printed in the United States of America

St. Martin's Paperbacks edition/November 1996

10 9 8 7 6 5 4 3 2 1

— PROLOGUE —

It reads suspiciously like the script of a Pedro Almodovar film: Popular foreign film star unknown in America rejects an internationally famous singer's flirtations, claiming to be a happily married man, only to later leave faithful wife for voluptuous blonde American actress after he becomes the English-speaking world's newest movie heartthrob.

Then again, Antonio Banderas's life has often played out like a movie—only before, he did it in the relative obscurity of Spanish cinema.

But since bursting onto the Hollywood scene, and into the hearts and libidos of female fans, as a doomed ex-patriot Cuban musician in *The Mambo Kings*, Banderas has been in the bright and occasionally uncomfortable spotlight. Some of it has to do with his intense screen presence but more of it can be credited to his suddenly spectacularly public private life. But as often has been the case, a white-hot career coupled with a red-hot romantic life is a formula that spells instant Hollywood stardom.

And downside notwithstanding, it's everything Banderas ever wished for.

ANTONIO BANDERAS

— CHAPTER ONE —

Antonio Banderas has been in love with American movies for as long as he's been in love with the idea of becoming an actor. In many ways, the two passions are inextricably entwined—the Yankee ideal that is communicated in our films hit many a foreign viewer as the epitome of artistic freedom.

"I first wanted to be an actor after I saw the movie *Hair*," Banderas has said, hands waving in memory. "Remember *Hair*? I saw it in 1974. I was fourteen years old. As soon as I saw it, I knew I wanted to do it. I was amazed—all those naked people. I wanted that American idea of freedom. Before that, I had only seen classical theater with my parents but when I saw *Hair* I thought, 'WOW!' This is *extraterrestrial*. Something about it got to me. It's like an American going to Spain and getting interested in bullfights. It wouldn't let me sleep at night. In the middle of the night I'd get anxiety attacks and I'd cry because I'd feel caught in my little world."

Obviously, the teenage Banderas was a particularly sensitive youngster in the first place to have such a strong emotional reaction to an otherwise mediocre movie musical.

"Well, yes," Antonio said earnestly. "I'd cry because I'd feel so incredibly . . . *impotent*. How could I ever be a part of something like *Hair*? Something that was crazy and hippie and wild and wanton? How could I be an actor if my parents were against it and my mother wanted me to lead a normal life? I felt that impotence of needing something and not knowing how to get it.

"When I saw that ritual, it was almost religious. I felt very anxious being only part of the audience. I wanted to be in the cast, leading different lives. So I decided to jump to the other side of the mirror. It actually made me start taking classes in theater and doing shows. I learned all the songs from the American musicals—*Singing in the Rain*, *The Phantom of the Opera*, *Guys and Dolls*, even *Evita*."

Banderas's parents must have thought they were in their own bad acid trip. Up to that fateful day when a flower-powered 60s musical rewired the synapses in Banderas's impressionable brain, Jose and Ana Banderas never dreamed their handsome son would chase after such an elusive dream. An unrealistic dream by their standards, not to mention very politically incorrect by Spain's then-standard. What had gotten into him?

Antonio grew up in the sleepily scenic Spanish city of Málaga, where he was born in the local Dieciocho Julio Hospital. Up to now Málaga has been best known for its sweet wine, resort beaches, and as the place where Picasso was born. Founded thirty-one centuries ago by Phoenician mariners and conquered by Carthaginians, Romans, Goths, and Moors, it was celebrated in Federico García Lorca's *Canto Nocturno*. It is a place at ease with its long and rich history.

Like the other boys coming of age in this coastal community, Antonio seemed unremarkable. He went swimming in the nearby sea and played soccer, one of his early passions. In fact, for a while he even toyed with the idea of pursuing a career as a professional soccer player—a dream that to his parents, at least, seemed more reasonable than being a big movie star. In America, no less.

"Antonio never dreams small, never has," says a friend, Walter. "Even when his thoughts were occupied by the image of being a soccer player, it was that he'd be the next Pelé. Whatever he was going to do, he'd do big. He'd be the best he could be. I think that's why he loves sports commercials in America. You know, 'Just do it.' That's Antonio."

To outsiders, young Antonio and his brother, Francisco Javier, enjoyed what would seem to be a fantasy upbringing but despite the beauty of the countryside, life wasn't completely idyllic for the youngsters. Not only did Antonio, who was born in 1960, spend his childhood in a country emotionally sagging under the weight of Franco's repressive ruling hand, things weren't always so comfortable at home, either. Jose worked for Franco's dreaded secret police, a job that was increasingly uncertain as the dictator's reign was coming to an end.

All in all, though, Antonio's father and mother Ana, who worked as a teacher, provided a stable home life. And what a family home. Up until he was well into school age, Antonio spent much of his childhood within the confines of a huge *terraza*.

"The house was very big so there was plenty of room for the boys to play," Ana has said. "They didn't have all that many toys—a few balls and some other things, but Antonio's favorite toy was a bucket he and his brother would fill with water and play in. Both the boys were happy children, and they played very well together—even though they were very different people.

"When Antonio got an idea into his head, nothing and nobody could make him change his mind. He's always been so *terco*. I remember there was one time Antonio wanted to go to bed with his boots on. It took me forever to finally talk him out of it and get him to take the boots off." Ana Banderas reportedly said, shaking her head and turning silent, smiling at the memory.

"But Francisco was just the opposite. He was a great compromiser. I think that's why they've always gotten along so well. They balance each other out."

Jose tried to keep the tensions of his work away from his family and once at home, he tried to be a regular Spanish Jose. And an attentive dad.

"My husband was always a very involved father," Ana Banderas recalled proudly. "He would always help me with the boys—changing diapers and feeding them. Antonio and his dad have always been very close, even when he was little. There was a natural bond.

"When Antonio was just a toddler, three or four years old, he would insist that Jose read him a story every night before going to bed. He called Jose *Pepe* and his favorite story was called *Pulgarcito*. Antonio had been read the story so many times, he knew it absolutely by heart. He would say, '*Pepe*, you made a mistake' if a part was read just a little bit wrong."

When Antonio was five, all chubby cheeks and thick dark hair, he started going to school. From the beginning, he had a naturally curious mind and nature, interested in everything and everybody. He was a popular student, friendly to the girls and ready to be rough and tumble with the boys. Even then, however, it was obvious Antonio was going to be a heartbreaker, his dark eyes highlighting an already handsome face.

Even if they weren't the most popular family on the block—little associated with Franco toward the end of the regime was welcomed with open arms—Antonio can still conjure up bright spots in what to him was mostly an uneventful and monochromatic childhood.

"I remember especially, during the summer, playing football out in the streets and never wanting to come inside," Banderas has said. "My mother would be calling me from the balcony, 'Antonio! Come to eat!' and I'd pretend not to hear her. I would drive her crazy."

But for an imaginative young boy growing up in balmy, sensual Málaga, the forbidden fruit of his youth was his dream of being a movie star. An idea that soon began to give his mother pains.

"Nobody in my family was in the theater. I'm the first one—I'm still the black sheep," he has said, only half kidding. "I was like a weird animal as far as my family was concerned. In the beginning, it was difficult for my family to understand that I wanted to be an actor. They told me I had to make a career, a *normal* thing. They made me feel as if I was doing something terrible *to* them."

And in many ways, he was. It cannot be overstated how shocking, even scandalous, the thought of such a career choice was for Antonio's parents. As a member of the secret police, Jose was sworn to uphold Franco's government and here was his son toying with the idea of pursuing a profession that was famous in Spain for being full of radicals and insurgents. Under the thumb of Franco, the government agenda was control of its people and as such opposing views and opinions were officially discouraged. It was a career choice of such fundamental significance for the Banderases that there was the very real potential for a severe, if not permanent, family rift.

"They made me think I was crazy," Antonio sighed, admitting he wasn't really appreciative of the political ramifications of his desire to act. "I'd lie in bed and think 'This must not be normal, wanting this. This makes no sense.' But yet it did. All I wanted was to try something for myself. It really had nothing to do with them."

Part of his family's horror was the abruptness of it all. One day they had a normal kid, the next minute they were living with the Iberian Norma Desmond, preparing for his close-up with destiny. Prior to *Hair*'s life-altering epiphany, Antonio's childhood dreams had a more modest flavor. At one time or another, he toyed with the idea of being a fireman, a matador, or even a veterinarian. But a foot injury ended whatever thoughts Antonio may have had about being the Spanish Pelé, so when the acting bug hit, he was wide open and ready for it.

But looking back, the appeal of acting seems obvious now. Acting was the only professional where he could continually be everything and anyone he wanted to be. There was so much wonder in the world, so many different and fascinating things you could do or people you could become, why stop with just one life? Why not try on dozens of different skins—all without having to let the world in on the secret of who Antonio really is.

"Acting is about hiding, isn't it?" Antonio mused. "I like the mask. You know, whenever I come on to a movie set to work, after I have makeup on I feel different, I feel *better*."

Even though he knew his parents weren't kidding when they said they were violently opposed to him pursuing the life of an actor, not to mention wearing makeup, Banderas could think of nothing else. Finally, after one too many nights crying, he gave in to the fire burning in his belly and let the familial chips fall where they may.

"If I wanted to be an actor, I just had to do it."

Antonio would sit for hours in front of the family's little black-and-white television, mesmerized by Spanish-dubbed Hollywood classics sputtering to life on the screen. It was magic. If he couldn't find encouragement and emotional support from within his family, he'd find it from others who'd walked the path out of Málaga before him.

"García Lorca was born not more than a hundred kilometers from my home and Picasso was born just two blocks away from my house." An-

tonio feels a kindred sort of pride for other Mála-
gans who set off to conquer the world.

Antonio started his career before he had permanent facial hair, at the self-assured age of fourteen. He started at the bottom, when he started
with the local theater. Theater was a world in
which Antonio could immerse and lose himself.

"Acting is like a gate through which you can
jump to the other side, the dark side of the moon,"
Banderas has said dreamily. "It was an like an irresistible adventure you couldn't pass up."

He was fearless—and a born ham. While the
play may be the thing, the applause is a close second for Banderas.

"When I began doing theater, I never thought I'd
have a film career," Antonio explained. "Even in
Spain. We thought theater was much better, a
much more serious art. Movies were something
cheap.

"In Spain, you don't have a Warner Brothers or
Disney studio. The government is the one who
pays to make movies. They approve everything—
your script, the cast you want to use, the location
where you want to shoot. You take everything to
the cultural minister. That's the way it was, and
actually, it's still the way it is.

"Even today, probably the only one who can really produce a movie independently in Spain is Pedro Almodovar," he said, referring to the popular

director who is probably the person most responsible for Banderas's career.

But long before Almodovar would provide the wind for Antonio's acting wings, Banderas was learning to act in a Málaga theater. From the moment he walked onto a lit stage, Antonio knew he was home and threw himself into acting with all the pure enthusiasm and joy that youth can hold.

"While other kids were into rock and roll, as a teenager I was all theater, theater, theater," Antonio recalled. "I studied the classics at the School of Dramatic Art and we were always in the truck, traveling from little village to little village performing. You learned to do everything—scenery, costumes, makeup, and lights. It was wonderful.

"I still remember how the theater in Málaga smells. It smelled old, ancient, and deep. Sometimes I can still smell it and all those old feelings come back.

"We did everything—musicals, Shakespeare, Greek tragedies, and Spanish farce. All under the guidance of Guillermina Soto, she was my first acting teacher and she was very, very old.

"But she was also great. It didn't matter what we were performing, she was *always* the lead, even if the character was a man. So here was this old woman, playing *Don Juan*. But she taught us what was important and it wasn't whether she was a woman playing a man.

"She said that acting was like opera. What's important in opera is the music, not who's playing it. 'If I am a man or a woman it doesn't matter, it's the music of *Don Juan* that people will see.' "

With financial help from a local countess who Antonio admits to flirting with, Banderas was able to organize his own acting troupe and together they set off and traveled the villages of southern Spain. They drove an old pickup truck with the scenery piled up in back, and put on performances right in the street.

"It was like that for five years," according to Antonio. "I learned everything they had to offer and then some. I was having the time of my life—up to then, anyway. Even when we had to use our own money, it was fantastic. You know, these people, I remember them from my heart. Because they represent to me where I am now. The people are the best memory I have from my youth and from my land."

Ana Banderas had hoped the harsh realities of theater life would sober Antonio up, but just the opposite happened—he'd become even more intoxicated with the actor's life. But her fears notwithstanding, the irreparable rift was averted precisely because of her son's tunnel vision. Even though he was performing anti-Franco plays in his theater group, Antonio simply wasn't particularly political. His point of performing wasn't to change society or make any statement about the powers that be—it was simply a chance to be onstage. Nothing more.

"Before the fall of Franco began, I had thought life was great because that was all I had known," Antonio explained. "I'd never been out of my country before. I thought, 'This is life. The cops are the cops, they can just beat you on the streets and nobody will complain.' That *was* life."

Which is not to say the teenage Banderas was oblivious to the political climate *around* him. He just chose to concentrate on the world of drama, where he could create his own world and not have to deal with real-life conflicts.

"When I began acting in Málaga, Franco was alive—his regime didn't fall until 1975 when I was fifteen, so we were doing theater against the government. We had the cops around us all the time, watching what we were saying onstage. It was a very ugly time. But I wasn't thinking at the time just to fight against Franco. I was just loving the theater itself.

"But the system was to control everybody. I remember once acting in a play in Málaga and seeing the cops waiting for us backstage. I remember how their helmets would shine in the light. When we were done with the play and the curtain came down, the actors would be told to go with them and we'd be taken in for questioning. We were living like that—and we didn't even realize how scary it was.

"Then suddenly, democracy came to Spain and I realized life could be different. But it took time for the Spanish people to realize their freedom and not be self-censors. Even now, twenty years since Franco's death, a lot of older people in my country think with that same frightened mind.

"What's interesting is that when Franco died, a lot of theater groups died right along with him.

"You have to remember that theater at that time meant something very special in Spain. When I started acting, we were doing theater against the regime, against Franco. It was part of a movement that was searching for democracy. After he disappeared, it turns out they were just punching the air."

As a hopeful nineteen-year-old, with Franco finally dead and buried, acting was still all Antonio cared about. There was no time to sit and ponder the shape of Spain's future political climate, he had a life to live. So when he graduated from the National School of Dramatic Art, Antonio had to follow the road he had paved for himself. Even though he says he was driven by an urge he had no control over, Antonio also admits it was disconcerting to be so possessed by his desire to act.

"By the time I began to wonder, 'Why am I an actor?' it was too late. It's like asking, 'Why am I living?' Well, you're living, you can't go back. Even today, I don't know why I'm an actor. It probably was an irrational decision. But ultimately, I knew one thing, that I really didn't want to do anything else. So all I could do was see it through."

— CHAPTER TWO —

"I know my life changed forever on August 3, 1980, which was the day I took my suitcase down off the shelf to leave home," Antonio recalled. "I packed very little, just a few things. My parents gave me a little money, about 15,000 pesetas, which is a very small amount of money, and I set off to Madrid."

Jose and Ana were not happy. It was never easy to see a child walk out the door to start his journey as an adult, but watching Antonio leave to go frolic with a bunch of other would-be actors added to the pain of uncertainty. Why, they asked, couldn't Antonio do something more stable, more worthwhile? Why couldn't he be more like his younger brother, Francisco, who was planning to become an economist? Or why not be a priest, like his uncle?

A priest? The handsome young man could only

smile. His parents would never change—until he proved to them that he wasn't chasing after misty rainbows. That he was doing something important. He said good-bye to his stricken parents and promised to write and call regularly. As he walked down the road, he felt a weight lifting from his shoulders.

"Suddenly, the air smelled better and everything seemed to be so crystal clear in my eyes, like I was seeing this road for the first time. I wanted to etch everything in my mind."

After the placidly paced life of Málaga, Madrid exposed the nineteen-year-old Antonio to what seemed like a blur of activity. The city swirled with color and ideas that were now running rampant since Franco's demise. People exchanged ideas in cafés and sitting around any of the beautiful fountains that grace Spain's capital. Even though the people of Madrid, to a certain degree, still embraced the Iberian abhorrence of too fast-paced a lifestyle, compared to his boyhood home Madrid was a place that never slept—except between two and four every day.

"I was lucky that I got to Madrid just at that moment when everything was exploding," Banderas has said. "When Franco died, there was an explosion in the art world of Spain that lasted into the 80s. It was called *La Movida*, The Movement. There were all these new designers, new directors, and young people working in music. Now that people were free to think out loud, the ideas wouldn't stop—it was a flood. The energy was incredible. Everybody became a little bit crazy."

Yet, walking through the city, Antonio felt the same conflicting emotions that tear at anyone who suddenly finds themself on their own. On one hand, to have absolute freedom, with no family looking over his shoulder made him almost lightheaded. The city was full of young people just like himself, ready to try anything. Young women were equally open and willing to try new experiences, especially when they saw Antonio's handsome face and heard his sincere words.

But on the other hand, once faced with the realization he could do anything he wanted anytime he wanted, Antonio felt a bit overwhelmed. The enormity of being responsible for finding your own way in life was like standing on the edge of a cliff. The knowledge that there was no one to disapprove of his actions waiting back at the small apartment he rented made him dizzy. He was in charge.

To keep himself centered and balanced, he put on some blinders most of the time. He concentrated on making his dream of being a professional actor come true and put most of his energies behind that goal.

And there was so much to learn. Prior to joining his theatrical group in Málaga, Antonio had seen acting very simply—you got up and spoke with your heart. It was emotion molded to fit the character you wanted to play. He was dumbfounded that people wanted to make it so complicated.

"When I enrolled in the School of Dramatic Art in my hometown, I got a real shock," Antonio laughed. "I'd never had the slightest idea of 'the Method' or of Stanislavsky. I didn't know those things even existed. For me, acting is a much more intuitive thing, much more direct."

So Banderas set out to find a place in Madrid where he could hone his craft the way he felt most comfortable. A place where his natural passion for life and people could be focused as an actor. He wanted to be a storyteller, but with his body as well as his words. Antonio had no idea how to start so he followed the time-honored tradition of hitting the streets and signing up for any audition he could find. And like so many others, Antonio quickly found it wasn't always easy opening new doors. For three years he worked at a variety of odd jobs—he waited tables in a pub, worked as a salesperson in a department store, and performed in no-pay experimental theaters.

"The money I earned went to buy decent clothes for auditions and to pay for acting lessons," he recalled. "I remember I couldn't even afford to take the bus, so I had to walk six miles to get to an audition. As I walked, I'd look between the parked cars hoping to find some change that someone might have dropped.

"It was probably the hardest time of my life, because I had moved from my family, from my land, I left behind my friends, my new house, everything," Banderas has said. "To make it that much worse, for a year and a half, I was without work."

It was an incredibly frustrating time for Antonio. Every time he watched television, he would think, 'I can do that!' If he could only get the chance. He would walk outside Madrid's theaters and envy those actors whose names graced the marquees. He felt like an outsider unable to open the locked gate.

But slowly, the doors began creaking open. That's because unlike so many others, Antonio's brimming self-confidence, which refused to be dampened by eighteen months of being rebuffed, was backed up by intense, raw talent. And it was fueled by a burning ambition that refused to be denied.

Finally, Antonio was cast in some small stage productions but it wasn't happening fast enough. So, unwilling to settle for anything less than the best, Banderas tried out for Spain's National Theater—and passed the audition. Over the next six years, Banderas acted in whatever they threw his way, from Brecht to American drama to the classics. There wasn't a role he was afraid to try. And with each performance, his reputation grew, first within the theater company, then later among Madrid's overall artistic community.

Meanwhile, back in Málaga, Antonio's parents kept waiting for their wayward son to regain his senses and come back home. But for Antonio, there would be no turning back and as the years passed, Jose and Ana slowly came to accept that Antonio was determined to follow his heart. And being practical in the way the Spanish are famous for, they realized it was better to go along with his decision than lose him. So even though they didn't understand his need for the applause, they came to accept it. And perhaps secretly begin to relish it. Ana began a scrapbook, carefully and lovingly pasting Antonio's stage reviews on the pages, marveling how her son had grown into a man.

Toward the end of his stay at the National Theater, Banderas starred in a string of highly praised productions that showcased his versatility and talent. The productions that crystallized his future included "Los Tarantos" by Alfred Manas; "Daughter of the Air;" "City and the Dogs," an adaptation of the Mario Vargas Llosa novel and Christopher Marlowe's Edward II of England.

Despite having found a measure of success at the National Theater, Antonio's sights had always been set much higher. The stage was merely a jumping-off point for grander dreams. Banderas didn't know when the opportunity would come to take the next big step so he worked feverishly to prepare himself so he'd be ready at a moment's notice. He intended on doing it all—film, theater and television. No medium would go unconquered.

One night in 1982, after a performance, the key to Banderas's big-screen future walked backstage.

But at the time, it merely looked like yet another starving *auteur*.

"I had been at the National Theater for about a year when one day someone told me, 'There's a young director here. Very modern, very strange. He wants to meet you,'" Antonio remembered that life-changing day.

At the time, nobody knew Pedro Almodovar—he was just one more aspiring Spanish filmmaker. But like Antonio, Almodovar burned with a desire to succeed, to see his odd imagery and ideas captured on film. He was intense and magnetic and Antonio felt his energy instantly.

"He was nobody then," Banderas recalled. "He had seen me in the play and came to the dressing room. He opened my dressing room door and walked in, this wild, dirty, underground director with a reputation for breaking all the rules. He asked if I wanted to make a movie. I said, sure, what's it about? He told me it was about a bunch of crazy people in Madrid.

" 'Wanna do it?'

"I read the script, then said yes."

Years of playing the struggling, dirt-poor actor had lessened Banderas's previous aversion to the cinema. Although this movie was like few films Antonio had ever seen.

In *Labyrinth of Passion*, the part Almodovar wanted Antonio to play was a gay Iranian terrorist whose most notable characteristic is a highly sensitive sense of smell.

"I thought, this guy is either crazy, or a genius. Luckily for both of us, he was both."

It was the beginning of a ten-year collaboration that would make both of them international stars. But in the beginning, it was more like a mom and pop operation than a future multimillion-dollar enterprise.

Almodovar ran his film company like a repertory theater group. With a little boot camp tossed in. Everyone was expected to pitch in and egos were not allowed—except for Pedro's. It was hardly the kind of pampering Banderas would come to know in later years, but it was the perfect training ground for an actor willing to take any risk.

"I started out doing movies with blood and sweat," Antonio laughed at the memory. "It was a big adventure. We'd begin a movie and we didn't know if we'd be able to finish because we didn't have enough money. It was underground, absolutely underground. We had no trailers—we were standing on the street, waiting there to shoot a scene. We were paid nothing.

"We never thought the films would be seen outside our frontier. In Hollywood, it's like a big factory that makes movies that they know will be seen around the world. But that wasn't our situation. We were lucky to be able to shoot more than one

lationships. He went from girlfriend to girlfriend, careful not to commit himself, but even so, whoever he was with at a given moment still felt she was the center of his universe. Needless to say, more than one surprised young lady thought she had won Antonio's heart only to have him leave and move on to the next pretty *señorita.*

Antonio liked them all, possibly even loved one or two, but there was something missing in each of them, something that kept him from losing his heart in the way he knew he could. He dated so many girls, he sometimes wondered if he even knew what or who he was looking for. While part of him loved being free to experience so many women, another part of him hoped he'd find that special person soon. He found the lightweight affairs and relationships were beginning to tire him. It was becoming an effort to maintain light and airy conversation. He wanted something deeper. He wanted to find that one person, the person written about in sonnets who shares your heart and soul as well as your bed.

"Unless a man has a woman with him, he is nothing," Banderas has said. "Having that special person is everything. At least I came to understand that. During my days at the National Theater, I thought I was happy—until I came to discover what true happiness was."

Antonio wasn't looking for love the moment when he lost his heart. He was simply looking to buy a cup of coffee in the café located below the National Theater. He walked in and stopped short, his heart abruptly pierced by Cupid's arrow at the sight of a petite, dark-haired woman with large eyes. It was at that moment that he suddenly realized what had been missing—and who he'd been waiting for.

— CHAPTER THREE —

Banderas is fascinated at the quirks of fate that control our destinies, like how a simple urge for a cup of coffee can end up changing your life forever. On the other hand, like the true hopeless romantic he is, Antonio also believes he was destined to meet his future wife—if not at the café that day, then somewhere else at another time. Their relationship was Kismet. But as it happened, it started with Antonio needing a strong caffeine fix.

"This coffee shop is very famous in Madrid and it's where all the actors and actresses meet and talk about the theater," Antonio explained. "I remember I was doing a Lorca play at the time. The moment I saw her, I immediately felt she was special. There was something about her that I immediately understood. I *had* to meet her."

Her name was Ana Leza, a fellow actor trying to

make her way in Madrid. Although Banderas didn't know her, Ana was well aware who he was when he walked over and said hello.

"She had seen the play I was doing and she loved it. And we started talking and talking and we kept on talking. We never stopped talking."

He insisted on having her phone number and called her immediately to ask if she'd go out to dinner with him. He whooped it up when he got off the phone, delighting in his own silliness. First dates are often exciting, but this was different. This was exhilarating. Antonio was burning down to his shoes.

Always one to act on his instincts, Antonio set out to win Ana's heart without giving it a second thought. They started a whirlwind courtship, one that brought out the true romance of Antonio's soul. He bought flowers, wrote poetry, and composed songs. He held Ana's hand as they took walks and talked late into the night, no subject taboo. Banderas believed he had found the person who listened to his heart as well as his words. He had found his special lady.

"Nine months later, we were married," Antonio smiled.

Because Antonio was so busy with the theater, he and Ana exchanged vows in Madrid in a simple ceremony attended by their weeping families. Antonio's parents immediately fell in love with Ana and embraced her as their own daughter. Antonio was equally welcomed into Ana's family. The newly merged families spent a wonderful day together celebrating with the bride and groom, who found it hard to be apart even for a moment. Friends of Antonio looked on with amazement—it was an unreal sight to see a former Casanova so helplessly in love. He seemed like a different person—and according to Antonio, he was.

"After meeting Anita, I was a much happier man. Before I had only thought I was happy when I was really just unconscious and crazy, having good times with my friends. Now I had someone I could share everything with, the good and the bad.

"I would tell my wife everything. Sometimes it was painful, especially if I had behaved badly, but fortunately I didn't have much time to be very bad. But there was a comfort in telling her everything. Complete trust is the only way."

1986 was turning into a bellwether year for Antonio. Not only had he married the woman he considered his soul mate, but his old friend Pedro Almodovar had lined up his first film to ever have a real budget. *Matador* would put Almodovar on the Spanish cinematic map, a road that Banderas would follow to movie fame as well.

In *Matador*, Banderas played Angel, a handsome, wealthy would-be matador. In the self-deluded way of the rich, Angel believes he loves danger so he goes into training to be a bullfighter. There's only one snag—he faints at the sight of blood. His instructor, a famous, retired matador is offended by Angel's lack of machismo and suggests that perhaps the rich mamma's boy is homosexual.

Confused and desperate, Angel, who is still a virgin, decides to prove his manhood. After putting on a red sweater, he attempts to rape the matador's beautiful young mistress. But as in everything else he does, Angel hasn't thought his actions through. The mistress, an aspiring model, knows Angel—and in fact, lives next door. After Angel bursts into her house, she's more curious about what he's up to than worried about her honor. She waits patiently while he fumbles with a pocketknife he's trying to hold to her throat. Unable to get the blade out, he has to make do with the corkscrew. When he is finally ready to do what he came for, Angel prematurely ejaculates.

The woman slaps him in contempt—it turns out this is the third time he's tried to rape her and failed. But when she turns to leave, she trips and falls, causing the hyper-sensitive Angel to faint. While passed out, Angel dreams about a series of murders and upon waking up, believes he's actually committed them. In *Matador*, Banderas is Almodovar's male version of *I Love Lucy*, daft and surreal.

Angel is so lost in his fantasies, he actually confesses to the murders he has dreamed about and it takes a smitten defense attorney to finally save the day—and his hide. In the end, it turns out that Angel is actually clairvoyant and has been "seeing" visions of others' crimes. It's a perverse slapstick that would become Almodovar's trademark. But Banderas plays it straight, refusing to patronize the hapless Angel.

"People took notice of that movie," Banderas has noted. "Almodovar just has a strong voice, it's hard to ignore his work, whether you like the films or not."

The gay theme that's only briefly touched upon in *Matador* was brought out for full frontal examination in their next collaboration, *Law of Desire*, in which Antonio is cast as a lonely boy with an obsessive homosexual desire for an avant-garde film director. Once again, Antonio's character is a troubled, privileged young man lusting after a cocaine-snorting director. Inevitably this fatal attraction leads to murder.

Reaction to the film, specifically Antonio's role, surprised Banderas.

"Everyone was asking me the same question— 'Why are you playing a homosexual?' I reminded them that the guy was a murderer but that seemed not to matter. It was amazing that playing a gay person was controversial when playing a killer wasn't. I'd see American and European movies with gangs and people killing people and nobody complained. But you play a gay character and people go off their heads."

Antonio did have a few private qualms about the

film, but not because he worried about what people would think of him doing an erotic gay love scene.

"I was a little scared after doing the love scene because I was afraid the movie might turn out to be bad. I got over the physical part pretty quickly, although at first, I must admit, the thought did go through my mind, 'God, this is disgusting,' about one of the rawer scenes. Then I went to the first rehearsal and it was so easy. So natural. I didn't lose my fingers, my ears didn't fall off—nothing will happen if you are sure of who you are.

"Even so, my role in *Law of Desire* was probably the most difficult I'd ever done. He was such a dangerous person, always bending toward death. That was the only escape he could find. And I must say, the acting was very hard. I think a movie like that was necessary for Spain, and for the rest of the world, too. It was a film that dignifies gay passion, just as it is, in the flesh.

"Yes, it was a tough movie because for Spain it was something completely new. It touched on all the taboos—homosexuality, drugs, and even people changing genders. Everything you can think of was put into the movie—and people who saw it accepted it. It was huge box office in Spain. So I think it was a good thing. But it did take a lot out of me."

However, Banderas's anxiety about the quality of the finished product didn't extend to what people

ANTONIO BANDERAS

may have thought of him for his shocking performance.

"It doesn't matter if people think I'm gay. I'm an
actor, not a censor. It was a wonderful script and
an unusual love story. I've always wanted to play
all sorts of people—gay, straight, good and bad.

"Kissing another actor felt normal. I am not a
homosexual but *Law of Desire* was a homosexual
story. I mean, *Total Recall* with all its violence is all
right but *Law of Desire* isn't? Kissing another man
is a big no-no, but kids can see blood splashed all
over the screen and it's fine? In America, anything
sexual is a sin in the Midwest? Are we crazy?"

Then Banderas smiled. "Sometimes, I like to be
a devil."

But there was an unexpected result from *Law of
Desire*'s graphic depiction of gay sex, one that gave
Banderas his first exposure to the dark side of
fame.

"A guy got my phone number and was leaving
scary messages on my answering machine after the
movie came out," Antonio said quietly. "Continually, for a couple of months, he was calling and
telling me, 'You don't know me, but I know you.
I'm gonna find you and take you behind some corner.'"

Interestingly, Antonio couldn't tell whether the
guy was going to beat him up out of disgust over
Banderas's portrayal of a gay man on-screen, or
wanted to show Antonio a good time. Either was

a frightening scenario and for the first time Banderas realized the impact a film and its actors can have on an audience. Suddenly, he wasn't just a character, he was a real person who spoke intimately to people in the privacy of a darkened theater. Most people easily separate character from actor, but for others the line blurs and for someone like Banderas, it can bring unwanted and unintended attention.

"From then on, I was watching behind me a little bit all the time. Especially at night if I was going somewhere alone. Someone crazy can come to your city, watch you, find out things about you and scare you really badly. But after that it stopped—there was nothing more."

There was no denying that Banderas *was* a sex symbol who appealed to men apparently as much as women. He was the kind of movie star who women love and who men wanted to be like. But Banderas never threatened other men with his looks; instead, he downplayed them and made fun of them.

"Every morning when I wake up, I look in front of the mirror and it says 'sex symbol.' Once I see that, I go back to bed," Antonio once joked with a journalist. But in all seriousness, it's important for him that others see him as a regular guy, a guy with substance, not just pretty packaging.

"When I am not acting, I am thinking about acting. But overall, I am a very regular person. I like to watch TV, read books, and travel. I like football—not American football, but soccer. And tennis is also great, because all you have to do is call one friend up and you can play. Soccer needs twenty-two people, so it's not as easy getting a game together.

"But to me, reading is the most enjoyable thing to do. I think I can find a lot of things about myself in books that I can later put into my movie characters."

In 1988, Almodovar released his most popular film to date. *Women on the Verge of a Nervous Breakdown* was a runaway hit in Spain and was given the honor of being screened the opening night of the Cannes Film Festival. The farcical story revolved around a woman nearly driven mad when she's spurned by her middle-aged lover. By Pedro's standards, not exactly a shocking plot. So not too ironically, many critics who had embraced Almodovar for his outlandishness, considered this movie the director's least clever work to date. But its accessibility to the masses gave Almodovar new clout and made Banderas a national name—despite the actor having a relatively small role as a wimp who hides his face timidly behind some very unhunk-like glasses.

Life had settled into a comfortable, familiar routine. When he wasn't working for his old friend Almodovar, Banderas was filming movies with other European directors and appearing in high-profile television projects. His future as a Spanish star seemed secure and he enjoyed the fruits of his labor. In between jobs he and Ana would travel, eating fine food and drinking expensive wine. One of the bigger ironies for Banderas was his sudden affinity for his hometown. The same place that had constricted him as a child now beckoned to him with a primitive siren's song.

"Knowing Antonio, it was a combination of things," says a longtime friend. "On one hand, there really is a comfort going back to the land of your birth, to the streets you know so well, the smells, the feel of the wind, all the things that give you continuity as a person.

"Then on the other hand, Antonio could go back home with a well-earned sense of vindication. When he had left to be an actor his parents were terribly upset that he was trying to catch the wind so it's fair to say that one thing Antonio enjoyed so much about coming home was the success-is-the-best-revenge aspect to it."

They were one big happy family and Antonio was their golden child so when he and Ana came for visits they were fussed over and pampered. They would spend the days lazing on the shore of the Mediterranean watching the sky turn into lightly painted pastels as dusk approached. Lying under the Spanish sky, Antonio would let his mind wander, his dreams drifting over the nearby water. At times, nothing seemed impossible. Ana, on the other hand, worried where Antonio's dreams might lead them, but if Antonio was aware of her concerns, he didn't let on.

When *Women on the Verge of a Nervous Breakdown* became an art-house hit in America, nobody was more excited than Antonio. America was the land of movies, the celluloid Mecca of the world. Nobody did movies better than the Americans—they had invented it. Other cultures had adapted films to fit their people, but Americans and movies were a natural love affair.

"Whether they admit it or not, every European actor wants to be in the American movies," Antonio has said. "And anyone who denies it is a liar."

The film earned an Oscar nomination for Best Foreign Film for 1988. Almodovar, delighted at the honor, gathered up his troupe and they all set off to Los Angeles to attend the Academy Awards in March 1989.

"That was the first time I ever came to Los Angeles," recalled Antonio, still wide-eyed at the memory. "Since Pedro always worked with the same people, all of us knew each other like brothers and sisters and we traveled as a group. It was like going off to camp. We were absolutely giddy, like kids.

"You have to understand that we were just a bunch of actors coming from doing these low-budget movies and suddenly we won a prize in some European festival and it became bigger and bigger and bigger and then, boom, we were in America for the Oscars. The exciting thing for us at the time was just seeing the stars. The whole group went to the Oscar ceremony and we were like, 'Oh, look there's *Gene Hackman*.' 'Guess who I just was in the bathroom with ... *Karl Malden*. I was just standing at the urinal with Karl Malden.' We were just crazed."

In an ironic foreshadowing that only happens in real life because it would be too pat for movies, Banderas was introduced to an actress he knew from seeing her movie *Working Girl*—Melanie Griffith.

"She was up for Best Actress and I remember thinking she was very beautiful." To prove he wasn't blowing hot air, he even described what she was wearing.

"She had on a white dress with pearls. For some reason that stuck in my mind. But then she moved on and I went back to staring at all the other stars there. It was a strange, strange experience. I remember looking out from the stage at the Oscars seeing Liza Minnelli, Jack Nicholson, and Kevin Costner, thinking, 'What am I *doing* here? This is not my place.' I didn't even know who Sharon Stone was because I had never seen any of her pictures, not even *Basic Instinct*.

"It's funny, sometime later we did a champagne commercial together so I got a chance to meet Sharon and now I know very much who she is. She is smart, funny, an incredible beauty, and controversial. I tell you, she is the perfect person to work with Almodovar. He would flip for her.

"But at the time of the Academy Awards, I was lost. To tell you the truth, the only thing I could focus on was that I had bought a pair of new shoes and couldn't bear the pain. My wife and I went to the party afterward and I met John Singleton and Spike Lee, people I really like. But instead of enjoying the moment, all I could think was, 'I either have to leave or take off these shoes, but if I take them off, I'll never be able to put them back on again.'

"That Hollywood stuff, cameras flashing, people in the stands screaming, 'Aaaargggghhhh!' is circus craziness. It's fun to play with, but that's all it is. Afterward, I thought that at least I had the chance to experience it and it would be something I could one day tell my grandchildren about. You know, 'Once, a long time ago . . .' "

Because he was so in awe of the bigger-than-life goings-on around him, it never occurred to Antonio that there may have been some people at the Oscars looking at him. Much to Antonio's surprise, host Billy Crystal singled him out as the new sex symbol who would replace Richard Gere. Plus there were others already thinking Antonio's time in America was at hand.

"There was a guy working at ICM named Emanuel Nunez and he wasn't even an agent yet. But he was very sharp and very ambitious," Banderas has said of two traits he would easily recognize in others because it also described him. Later, Nunez would become his American agent.

"Emanuel knew that Arne Glimcher and Warner Brothers Studio were preparing a movie called *The Mambo Kings*. So Emanuel tells me about it and says, 'It's a great Spanish character and I think you should get an interview with the director.' He was very earnest and well-intentioned but there was a fatal flaw. I told him that I didn't speak a word of English. Not one.

" 'This would be ridiculous,' I told him. But there was also another thing going on in my head," Antonio admitted. "I suddenly got very frightened. So I used language as an excuse. The thought of actually doing an American movie caught me off guard and was too scary to deal with. So I just thanked him and tried to forget about it."

Banderas returned to his life in Spain and the excitement of being in Hollywood and a part of its glamour slowly faded into a warm, fuzzy memory. The thought of what might have been never fully evaporated, leaving its enticing residue on the outer reaches of Antonio's mind. But work kept Banderas too busy for dwelling too much on fantasies. On the heels of his last triumph, Almodovar was readying another film. Although Antonio could not possibly know it, it would be their final collaboration for a long time to come.

— CHAPTER FOUR —

*T*ie Me Up! Tie Me Down! was a mixed bag for all concerned. And a lesson of how a little success can ruin a good thing.

"Before, we just sort of worked in obscurity, just a group of people making a movie," Antonio has said thoughtfully. "But once *Women on the Verge* became an international hit, everything changed. The stakes got higher for all of us. I think there was now an expectation that Pedro had to live up to. Not in his eyes, necessarily, but in the film community's eyes. Or at least *he* thought so. And I think it is possible there were more expectations of me as well.

"But in any event, thinking about it now, I think there would have been a lot of tension anyway simply due to the nature of the film."

Tie Me Up! Tie Me Down! is a perverted love story

about handsome, young mental patient Ricky, played by Banderas, who is obsessed with a porno movie star named Marina. Ricky decides to kidnap the erotic actress and hold her hostage until she gives in, comes to her senses and falls in love with him in return. Which, typically in Almodovar's universe, she does, but only after Ricky is beaten to within an inch of his life by dastardly drug dealers.

"The story was very claustrophobic," Banderas has said. "We were cooped up in one house, one soundstage, day after day after day. With poor Victoria Abril, who played the actress, tied to that bed the whole time. It was so hot that summer and with the cameras constantly circling us, there were times you felt faint. Physically, it was a very difficult, almost painful, film to film."

Banderas admits that whenever he worked with Almodovar, the lengthy scenes in bed eventually wore thin, regardless of how innovative or erotic they were. Not because of what they depicted, but because of the intensity with which they were filmed. No one could function at full acceleration all the time—you needed to idle every now and then.

"They were tough, very tough scenes to do," Antonio sighed. "I know, as a kid you think, 'Wow, I'm getting paid to stay in bed all day, what a good job.' Except it wasn't so easy. They were very hard to do and to tell the truth, there were times when

I felt a little dirty. But that wasn't important at all, because that sensation of dirtiness was a *moral* sensation and morality doesn't go well with art. Working with Pedro in general isn't easy.

"People in Spain—and I only say Spain because when I was working with him that's where he was best known—people think working with Pedro Almodovar is a party. It is not. Pedro is very tough and very straightforward about it. He's the kind of person who'd rip the skin off your body to see what's going on inside.

"He's a very disciplined guy, even a little bit cruel. He'd sometimes say to me, 'Antonio, you sound so fake today. What happened to you last night? Didn't you sleep well?' But I like that. I like going to the set to sweat, to suffer a little bit, to discover things about yourself.

"Many actors are insecure and wait for the director to tell them what to do. I like to bring my own ideas to the set and I like to fight with the director if it's possible. That's the way you create art. Pedro wants the actors very fresh. For each take he wants something new, something different. We are like bullfighters. *Venga! Arriba! Ay!* Pedro creates an incredible, entertaining atmosphere. He's always making us laugh at ourselves. And when the day is over, we are always stunned by what we've accomplished."

Antonio took a puff from his cigarette, arranging his thoughts through wafts of smoke.

"Almodovar can also be very difficult. He is the owner of his films and if you want to introduce ideas, you have to be very smart. Very sly. You can't just say, 'I was thinking . . .' because he'll say you're not allowed to think. *He* is there to think. When you want to introduce ideas, you have to play games with him all the time.

"I think Pedro is the representation of European cinema. And there it's the director who is *Führer* when making a movie. Almodovar takes that role very seriously and is very demanding. He knows totally what he wants and he leads the whole thing. Not only the acting but the cinematography, lights, sound—everything.

"But I was always thankful to him for being tough with me. It's like a therapy in a way. Pedro and I always got along very well and my friendship with him is a brotherly friendship. And like brothers, we fight and have disagreements. And disappoint each other. But he sees something of himself in me which is why he picked me to be his alter ego on film.

"Almodovar is a breaker—he broke the structure of Spanish cinema. When he arrived, he gave the audience something new, something different, and something very courageous.

"In his movies, he's crying to the people, yelling to the people, daring them to be part of something aggressive. Yet, at the same time, he has a wonderful, beautiful sense of humor, too. He can tell you the harshest, most uncomfortable story and suddenly you are laughing and crying at the same time."

Understanding that in Europe it's often the director's name that sells movies explains why an artist like Banderas envied his American counterparts.

"Actors in America are more the owners of their work, I think, because they are the stars. The stars are the people who are selling movies and they have to be allowed their opinions on the script. This is something that I find very valuable."

As in his other films, Almodovar places a great emphasis on the craziness and insanity of the human soul in *Tie Me Up! Tie Me Down!*—something that Banderas has said is more than the director's cinematic style.

"For example, I know Pedro believes I'm a guy with a lot of turbulence in my head." Antonio laughed. "He believes I'm tormented. Am I? No— at least it is less than what he thinks, and for different reasons. Am I as tormented as Ricky? No. I hope not," he laughed again.

Despite Ricky's unorthodox approach to courtship, Antonio has said of all the Almodovar characters he played, he empathized the most with the young lunatic who is a prisoner of his love for a woman. And listening to an analysis he offered of Ricky shortly after the film's release, one senses Antonio is also being more than a little self-reflective.

"There was something profoundly animalistic

about Ricky," said Banderas in a soft growl. "He's enraptured by this woman and he *must* make her fall in love with him, no matter what. Even though he can get violent, I believe Ricky is a good person and in the deepest sense of the word, an innocent. There's nothing hypocritical about Ricky. He plays in an arena of truth. And truth, finally, gives him recompense.

"We're not sure of the price he'll have to pay for his truth—but it's probably a very high price."

Banderas shrugs off the charges that the film is wildly sexist and misogynistic.

"It is a double standard," he replied evenly. *"Tie Me Up! Tie Me Down!* was X-rated because I play a lovesick man who kidnaps a woman—and then she falls in love with him. Well, Disney's *Beauty and the Beast* told exactly the same story and even kids could see that.

"You know, there's something about Ricky that reminds me of Tarzan," Antonio asserted, drawing yet another American movie analogy. "One day I was watching television and I came upon one of those Tarzan-and-Jane movies. I thought about the possibility of the feminists attacking Tarzan for the way he treats Jane, because Tarzan grabs Jane, he hits her a couple of times, she faints and then he carried her up his tree. And when he gets her up there, he ties her up with vines."

Banderas seems genuinely taken aback when it's suggested that feminists have indeed attacked Tarzan as less than a sensitive, modern kind of guy. He listens intently to the main gripe—that the image of a woman being tied up against her will, a woman being force to submit to a man against her will isn't very sporting, not to mention extremely hurtful to feminine self-image. Woman as victim is a tired premise.

Banderas nodded, but wouldn't ante up.

"It's easy to criticize *Tie Me Up! Tie Me Down!* in a knee-jerk fashion. It's an escape for the critic to reduce and summarily dismiss the film as chauvinistic. It's easy to escape the film, too. You know, for people to understand the film, they must understand the most important line in the film is when the woman asks Ricky to tie her up. That's the moment she takes charge and stops being a coward. And it's then when she sees that she actually loves Ricky. Before that she was being blinded by reason—the same reason that makes people critical of the film."

And if there's one constant in Almodovar's films, it's that passion and love are beyond reason—they are the purest, and most primitive, expression of who we are as humans.

What nobody argued about was Banderas's animal magnetism on the prowl in *Tie Me Up! Tie Me Down!* And that pleases Antonio, because of his inherent compassion for Ricky.

"I love this character, I feel very close to him. Not that I would ever tie a woman to a bed, but that's probably because I would be scared—I'm not as valiant as Ricky."

Banderas found himself in a similar predicament of wanting something so passionately, but being too frightened to go for it. Except in this case it wasn't the love of a woman that held him at bay—it was the dream of being a true star, a *Hollywood* star. At first glance, such a thought really was the impossible dream, as a brief glance at movie history could attest.

Other than silent screen star Valentino, foreign-born actors have tended to be relegated to villains or colorful sidekicks. Especially a non-British actor. A true dramatic leading man who speaks with a discernible accent was uncharted territory so Banderas had every reason to be terrified. Wanting something that seemed to be a recipe for surefire disaster was a career death wish. But Antonio also knew in his heart he would never, ever be truly satisfied with his career if he didn't try to conquer American cinema.

"Antonio is ambitious in the broadest sense of the word," says an acquaintance. "Once he sets his sights on something, it becomes almost a matter of honor to succeed—at any cost. It's closely tied in to his national machismo, that if you work hard enough, you will succeed—nobody will stand in your way. The trick is to find the right way. Antonio realized he had to make the American people love him and see him as an all-American boy who just happens to be from Spain.

"Even though his film roles may be dark and broody, he instinctively knew Americans love a good laugh. If he ever got the chance, he'd win them over through humor and charm."

His opportunity came sooner than even Banderas expected it to but it would come with a Hobson's choice, one that would force Antonio to leave behind much of what he knew best in the world. But before he came to that particular fork in destiny's road, Antonio was formally introduced to American movie audiences via a most unlikely source—Madonna.

During the filming of Madonna's "rockumentary" *Truth or Dare*, which was originally going to be called *In Bed With Madonna*, Banderas became the object of the singer's desire when she announced on film that of anyone, Antonio Banderas was the one man she'd most like to go to bed with. The comedy of errors that followed did more for Banderas's future career in America than anyone, even he, could have imagined.

It began when Madonna, appearing in Spain, made arrangements for Banderas to attend a party she'd be at postperformance. Getting ready for her big moment, Madonna waxed poetically, if a bit raunchily, about her Latin dream boat.

"Is that man beautiful or what? There's got to be something wrong with him. He probably has a small penis or something. My God! There *has* to be something wrong with him because nobody can be that perfect."

But there was an unexpected snag—Antonio brought his wife Ana with him. When Madonna spotted Mrs. Right on the arm of Mr. Right, she went into a bathroom and sulked as if she had just endured the most humiliating rejection possible.

"I can't *believe* he brought his *wife*," she moaned. "This is a disaster."

Banderas has offered his side of the encounter.

"The real thing that happened was, I went to Madonna's concert in Madrid even though I couldn't speak English, hardly at all," he has told an interviewer, smiling cagily. "Anyway, I was at a table at a party Pedro gave and I saw cameras, but I thought it was the TV news, you know? I never felt she was going to do a movie. I mean, she never put a piece of paper in front of me asking if I wanted to be in this documentary.

"During that dinner she was telling me, oh, I don't know what, but the whole time I'm just smiling and nodding, saying yes, yes, yes—even though I didn't really understand a word she said. When someone called and said I was in Madonna's movie, I said it was impossible.

"But then she called me and told me not to be worried because I was treated like a king in her movie. She promised to send me a cassette and said if I didn't like what I saw, she'd take it out of the movie. So when Ana and I saw the movie and heard what she said about me, we just laughed and laughed.

"Until *Truth or Dare*, I was known in America only as Pedro Almodovar's actor by people who went to foreign films. Then I was the guy in *Truth or Dare*," Antonio laughed. "It was a joke—but also free advertisement—it was like a free two-page advertisement in *The New York Times*. Afterward, everyone was asking. 'Who *is* this Antonio Banderas?' I was definitely better known after that. Ana and I were thankful to Madonna for that. If a woman thinks you are sexy, good, I'll kiss her. But I *was* a happily married man and I needed to make that clear, too."

He wanted to keep peace in his household. His recognizability had begun to infringe on some of his private time with Ana, who was less sanguine about the intrusion than Antonio. But as his fame and career grew in Spain, it became harder to go anyplace without fans gathering around or a gaggle of love-struck girls following them down the street, their stage whispers expressing their undying infatuation for Banderas. Everywhere Antonio and Ana went, it seemed hordes of lovesick fans eventually gathered, like pigeons chasing after falling bread crumbs.

"You know how it is, you'll be walking down the street and you'll hear somebody ask, 'Is that Antonio Banderas?' 'No, it can't be, he's much shorter than that.' 'No, it is him—he just looks taller in real life.' But it's okay. Artists, I think, are more a part of the normal public in Madrid. I'd see the biggest stars out at restaurants without any hassle. I can go into the street, to the supermarket, pretty much anywhere and it's fine. Only if I go into a big store will people ask me for my autograph. But they are very nice and very complimentary."

Still, Antonio carries the added attraction of being his country's best known and most lusted after sex symbol, a fact that occasionally caused Ana some discomfort. So Antonio tried to shield her from it as much as possible, in an attempt to protect her and also to keep himself out of uncomfortable situations. For example, Banderas made it a rule Ana was never to visit the set of his movies the day a love scene was filmed.

"Never, never! It's one thing to be a professional and do your work, it's another to play games. I wasn't going to have my wife there because the other person could get violent. Like in *Tie Me Up! Tie Me Down!* Victoria Abril was such a nice actress. We were very generous with each other, the way we could touch each other. But at one point I thought, 'Maybe she'll punch me if I do this.'

"You know, it's not as much fun as you think, these sex scenes. The makeup artist is going over you all the time and there are fifty other people in the room. You have to stay in bed eight hours, sweating like hell, and it's very tiring. You always finish totally exhausted.

"Ana is very intelligent and she has an incredible sense of humor," Antonio added for no apparent reason. "You know, I can truly make love to someone when there's only one person in the room."

Many who had known Antonio in his younger days marveled that his marriage to Ana had lasted and still seemed so stable, despite his career having exploded the way it had. Even Banderas has acknowledged that his wistful side for a true one-on-one love had fought his lover-boy side. Although he has joked in interviews that he was practically a monk before meeting Ana, the truth is Antonio played the field in a big way.

"I tended to have a lot of girlfriends, it is true," Banderas admitted. "I love all women and found myself attracted to many women. After meeting Ana, some of my friends bet that our marriage wouldn't last a year. But they didn't understand that once I gave my heart, I would do my best to make it work."

The strongest thing the Banderases had going for their marriage, it would turn out, was their homeland. If Ana ever worried about her husband's faithfulness or lack thereof, their culture provided that the husband almost always returned to the wife. Affairs of the loins were tolerated in Catholic Spain much more so than divorce ever would be. In the practical manner of European women, what

Ana cared about the most was that at the end of the day or the end of the film, Antonio came home to her.

"In Spain, they were on mutual ground, equals in many ways even though Antonio's career was far more stellar," says a family friend. "Ana was gold with Antonio's family, she and her husband shared a long history and even when his work took him somewhere else in Europe, it was just a short flight away.

"Because he so often worked with Pedro, that company of actors had become extended family so it was all very cozy and comfortable.

"Make no mistake, Ana was comfortable with Antonio being a Spanish film star. Yes, the fans could get irritating and so could being interrupted when out in public, but ultimately, the fans were polite. And in truth, it made her proud to be on Antonio's arm because he had achieved so much. As long as she could keep him close by, everything would be all right."

What Ana feared was Antonio's restless spirit and his ambition to literally conquer the world. When he finally did get that chance, it would later prove to be the beginning of their end.

— CHAPTER FIVE —

A year after Antonio's triumphant visit to the Academy Awards, he was working in Venezuela on an Italian movie, his life proceeding in what was now its expected paces. But fate took Banderas in her hand and gave his life a spin.

"When I got back to Spain from Venezuela, I got this urgent phone call telling me I had to go to London at once," Antonio recalled. "I had barely unpacked my bags from South America and I was dead tired so the thought of jumping right back on a plane was not exciting. So I asked what the rush was and they told me I had an interview with an American director."

Suddenly, Antonio perked up.

"Okay, for that I'll jump back on a plane. They had told me to read the book *The Mambo Kings* so I bought it to read on the plane. By the time we landed in England I was definitely interested."

The book, Oscar Hijuelos's Pulitzer prize-winning novel, is about musician brothers from Cuba, Nestor and Cesar, who leave their island for New York City in the 50s after the younger brother falls in love with the girlfriend of a murderous gangster. Knowing he will be killed if he doesn't leave Cuba, the woman lies and tells Nestor she doesn't love him, breaking his heart.

"I was immediately taken with the story," Banderas has said. "It was a love story of a group of people. A love story between two brothers, between one of the brothers and a woman he's never going to see again, between the younger brother's wife and his brother. It's also a love story of two men and a city, of two men with music, of the music and the audience. It was also the story of the love-hate relationship between the two brothers. It was a very intense story and yet there were moments of humor, too. I was captivated."

Having arrived just in time for the mambo craze, the two brothers are determined to emulate the fame and fortune of their idol, Desi Arnaz. Painfully, the closest they get is an appearance on *I Love Lucy* after elder brother Cesar crosses paths with a powerful gangster type.

In London, Banderas met with Arne Glimcher. Glimcher, who owns the Pace Gallery in New York, had never directed a film before but he made up in passion what he lacked in experience. But Banderas's time with Glimcher was unusual to say the least. Not only did Antonio not know English, Glimcher spoke no Spanish, so they communicated with hands and signals.

"We had dinner in London and I hardly understood what he was talking about. He spoke slowly, although it didn't help me understand a language I still couldn't speak," Antonio laughed. "Well, that's not totally true, I knew a few sentences of English from old Beatles' songs. So he tried to explain what he wanted with his hands. He talked to me for two hours—a big monologue. And even though I couldn't understand one word he was telling me, I kept making faces, going, 'Oh, yeah . . . of course, right, right, right.' It was like a comedy."

Glimcher's version of the events takes a slightly different spin.

"I flew to London to meet with Antonio," Arne—who had not been told Banderas spoke no English—has reported. "But he was very, very charming. He kept sort of grabbing my arm and laughing at all the right moments. But then I realized he really wasn't saying much of anything.

"About fifteen minutes into dinner, I turned to him and asked, 'You don't understand a word I'm saying, do you?' And he just laughed loudly and grabbed my arm. I knew then I had my actor," Glimcher laughed.

"Antonio just instinctively knew when to laugh—and how to seduce you. And he can seduce every woman, man, and dog on the planet."

"I left thinking it was hopeless," Banderas has said. "But to my surprise, two weeks later Arne called me from New York and asked if I could fly to America to make a screen test. *Yes!* Here I am, I cannot make a sentence and he's trusting me to audition for his movie. I was so grateful to this man because he's not a silly man but he trusted me. I don't know why he did, but I was very, very grateful."

Antonio knew this was the chance he'd been waiting for so he immediately hired a coach back in Madrid to teach him the part he'd be auditioning for phonetically, line by line. He worked relentlessly, practicing the sounds over and over until he was saying them in his sleep. Finally, the day came to leave so Antonio headed for New York underprepared but swimming with adrenaline.

"My part, that of Nestor, the younger brother, was the last to be cast, or so I thought," Banderas has said. "When I got to New York, I started working with Kevin Kline and Annabella Sciorra, who were going to play the parts of my brother and my wife. It was so scary, because I didn't understand what they were saying, *or* what I was saying.

"I had only learned the lines phonetically, not their meaning. And there were a lot of lines from a lot of different scenes. Quite often I'd be lost because the other actor is improvising something and you have no idea what he is saying."

In reality, *The Mambo Kings* was not Banderas's first foray into an English-speaking role. In 1990, Antonio was asked to appear in a film called *Love and Shadows*.

"That's true," Banderas acknowledged. "Betty Kaplan, who is a Venezuelan director who was born in America, called me to do the film. She was directing a script based on the novel by Isabel Allende. And when they called to have me do the film, they did insist I learn a little English. But it was only a little because the movie eventually didn't get made so what little I learned, I forgot right away.

"The thing about English, though, is that it's a very practical language. It's great for business, for negotiations, for all those official kinds of things. And it's good for an actor to work in English because you can say a lot with very few words. But then again, Spanish is better for conversing with God."

After auditioning with Kline and Sciorra, Glimcher enrolled Banderas in a Berlitz school for the next month to learn English to see what kind of progress he could make. Antonio shook his head and laughed at the memory.

"I was in this class with a bunch of business executives from Japan and France. I saw people crying there—like me—because we thought we'd never be able to learn this language. But when you have to learn, you do. I had so much I needed to explain and it's frustrating when you don't have the words. So I made sure I learned the words.

"One month later it was time to audition again, but it was now very different. The two original actors I had worked with were gone. Now it was Armande Assante and Maruschka Detmers and it was so different. But good. Armande Assante played my brother Cesar, who is a very good showman, very ambitious, and I play Nestor, who's the real artist. Nestor has trouble expressing himself unless it's through his music. We clicked and it was then that I just *had* to get this role. I knew it was so close.

"But first, I had to go and audition—and speak—in front of all these big executives at Warner Brothers. I even forgot Spanish, if you can believe it. It was all so strange. I would use a word like *bottle* and think to myself, 'What a strange word that is.' But it was one of the most beautiful experiences of my life because of what I was able to overcome."

Finally, one Sunday after yet another long reading with twenty-eight actors, Glimcher called Banderas into his office.

"He said, 'Well, Antonio, I'm going to take a risk with you. I'm going to offer you the movie.' The day he told me I got the part, I went jumping from Forty-fourth Street to Greenwich Village. *Boing, boing, boing, boing.*"

Banderas ran along the streets, his arms raised

in a Rocky victory salute, while Manhattanites looked benignly on.

"I kept yelling, 'I'm going to make an American movie!'

"You have to understand, I was always a fanatic about American movies—I love George Cukor, Orson Welles, Raoul Walsh, Billy Wilder. Seeing Americans using washing machines in the 40s—the first washing machine my mother bought was in the 70s. Watching American movies was like a dream of a faraway world.

"To work in the big studios after watching American movies since I was a kid was a dream come true. It was like working in Disneyland. Here, the movies are done with money and that's the way they have to be done."

But Banderas's joy at landing a role in *The Mambo Kings* was tempered by a scheduling conflict. There was a film he'd have to pass up to make his American debut. But it wasn't just any film. Pedro Almodovar—his mentor, the man many say is responsible for his career—was readying his new film, *High Heels*. Antonio was left with the unpleasant task of telling Pedro he wouldn't be available. Almodovar already had a reputation for being an unforgiving director toward other actors who had left the fold to move on to higher-profile projects. Not surprisingly, Almodovar thought Banderas was selling out.

It wasn't that Banderas had never worked for another director, quite the contrary. But it wasn't just a matter of working with another director. They both knew Antonio wanted to be a Hollywood movie star, speaking a language other than his native tongue. Going to Hollywood, conquering that golden land, was what Pedro knew Antonio was really going for. That was the reason he would choose *Mambo Kings* over Almodovar.

"You know, I had worked with Pedro for a long time, we grew up in our careers together," Antonio explained. "We did five films in ten years. I wasn't thinking, 'OK, it's time to break away from this working relationship.' I simply decided to take another step, breathe new air, fly away, and know other people. And Hollywood, all around the world, is *something* for an actor. As it is for a director," he added pointedly.

"So, I went to his home one night in Madrid and told him, 'Listen Pedro, they've offered me this film and I want to do it.' He was disappointed. So was I. I knew he couldn't tell his team of forty, fifty people, 'We'll have to wait for Antonio.' So he cast Miguel Bose in the part I would have done. And Miguel was great.

"At the beginning it was a little bit hard between us but a couple of days later he called me and said, 'Antonio, we are going to work together in the future.' We were like gentlemen. Nothing was broken. Pedro gave me a picture of him and me in New York that he signed 'Mambo Kings play sad songs.' We still talk by phone and are still friends."

Not only was parting with Almodovar bitter-sweet, it was like leaving home a second time. Starting over with the same insecurities and doubts.

"When you work with the same people over and over again, you do become like a family," Antonio said with feeling. "It was so much fun. And because we knew each other, we didn't have to deal with new life histories, new personalities. Julieta Serrano is my mom in one film, then she's my mom again in another. And Carmen Maura, oh what a gorgeous girl."

Maura and Banderas have acted in six films together and they have played lovers, siblings, stepson and stepmother. He considers her one of his closest friends and his movie "everything."

"I can't describe Carmen. She's a fantastic actress and a wonderful person. When you see her on the screen, she is very strong, very independent, very tough—and at the same time, very sweet, fragile, and tender. Carmen is intuition, absolute intuition. She works with her *skin* and I learned so much from her.

"These are people I love so it was hard to make the decision not to work with them. But I knew I had to see what this other world held for me.

"I hope to work with Pedro again. If he needs me, he'll call. We are very young people and I am sure we will work together in the future. But" —Antonio reportedly paused. "If we never work together again . . . well, we've done many beautiful films together over the years and that's enough for me."

But letting go is never easy and Banderas admited it was difficult attending the opening of *High Heels* as a mere observer.

"It was a very strange sensation to go with my wife, Pedro, and Miguel to the premiere of the film in Madrid. Opening nights of Pedro's movies all over Europe are big events. You see, everybody thought Almodovar would have power a year or two, but not forever. But Pedro is smarter than that. A problem we Spanish have is that only when someone becomes celebrated all over the world do we recognize them as well. That happened with Pedro. Picasso, too.

"So, I had been with him to the last consecutive five premieres. But at this one, it was all about Pedro, Miguel, Victoria Abril, and the very good work *they* had done together. So there was a kind of sadness. There was a change happening. I was ending a time that would never come again. But the sadness didn't last long because *The Mambo Kings* was coming. That's what I needed to concentrate on."

Interestingly, *The Mambo Kings* brought to light a little known secret love of Antonio—he was a closet musician. He loves playing the guitar and piano and even had a recording studio built in his Madrid home. So he says he understood the musician's soul of Nestor. But mastering that trumpet was something else.

"I only ever learned to mimic playing the trumpet," Banderas has said. "There was no way to learn to really play it. It is a very difficult instrument. And even mimicking playing is hard. It's very difficult to get your lips in the right position so that it will look like you're actually playing. That was almost as difficult as learning English."

Preparing for *The Mambo Kings* was nothing like Antonio had ever tried before. It required more concentration than he thought it possible for someone to muster. For a self-professed instinctive actor, *The Mambo Kings* required a strict, very material agenda, including an intense month in New York studying English at another Berlitz school for eight hours a day, three hours a day of trumpet and dance lessons, and then nights spent checking out the jazz and salsa clubs. Banderas personalized the role of Nestor in a way he never had before, aware of the ironic similarities between them.

"I was just like Nestor," Banderas has said. "I was new to this country and was experiencing the same struggles with the language and culture that he was. I *was* Nestor. I was learning English with Cubans around me. It was impossible not to get the accent so it was perfect. I could even use my own mistakes for the role."

But there was also a downside to his study.

"This movie is about the Spanish community in

the 50s in New York City. But it's mostly about the American dream," he said quietly. "Cuban immigrants arrived in this country and injected a new energy here. And I don't know why, but after the 50s, the Spanish culture seems to disappear in this country in some way—for those who aren't Spanish, that is. Rock and roll pushed it aside. Now, it has become popular again, through salsa and other stuff. But sometimes when working on this movie I asked myself the question, 'Why do Italian or other communities develop in this country more than the Spanish culture?' It's true. I don't know why but they are ghettoized more than the Italians and others."

At times, Banderas himself must have thought he was pursuing a pipe dream. But now that he was on the track, there was no way he could get off the train. It was a daring, risky move. Many of his friends and family didn't understand why Antonio would put himself in a position to fail. At thirty-one, Banderas had made almost thirty films and was a big fish in the European film community. And yet in America, he was still just the guy in *Truth or Dare*.

"Yes, it's true, I had been playing leading characters in Europe for six years before I came to America for *Mambo Kings*," Banderas has said. "Of course I had to sacrifice a lot of things that I was already doing in Europe. But I knew I had to accept that. Actually, *Mambo Kings* was a relatively big role, compared to the ones that came right after. In many of the movies, you blink and you missed me. But that's okay. I knew I would have to gradually build a career here, so I told my agents that I preferred to take smaller roles and work with really good directors and good actors, because I was starting over from the bottom.

"I don't like to have anything I don't deserve, it makes me really uncomfortable. I would like to be honest and I'd like to have integrity. Of course, I would also like to be successful, but only on those terms."

Even if Banderas's friends and family worried that he was throwing it all away, he was comfortable with his plan of attack. Now, his attention was turned to *Mambo Kings* and to get the role down he immersed himself in the Cuban community and became a student of the mambo and its curious cult following.

"First of all, the real *mamberos* hate the term salsa," Antonio has stated. "Mambo is the most sexual music in the world—and sexual in a way that *enjoys* sex. Flamenco is sexy but in flamenco you have to suffer. Tango is torture, too. But Mambo is sex to enjoy. Mambo is here, it begins here," Banderas has reportedly said, his hands above his hips, "and finishes here," his hands resting lightly on his thighs. "I mean, that's mambo! Mambo is to enjoy life."

Banderas spent six months working on *The*

Mambo Kings, and with each passing day he loved America that much more.

"As Cesar says in the movie, I was always saying, 'I LOVE this country.' On one hand, it was scary, almost like beginning all over. But on the other, I just had this sense that my future was here. Whatever happened, however the movie was received, taking this role was the right thing for me to do.

"*The Mambo Kings* changed my life. It was the beginning of me spending more time in America. In fact, since then, I've lived in America more than I have in my own country.

"Never, ever am I going to have the words to thank Arne Glimcher because of the way he trusted me and the way he took this risk. I think he was even more courageous than I was about it. If Pedro Almovodar was my mentor in Spain, then Arne Glimcher was the key in the door of my career here in America."

Working in another country was an eye-opening experience for Banderas.

"Knowing that this was Arne's first film sort of made me a little more comfortable, like we were together on a great new adventure," Antonio has said. "I remember sitting in rehearsal and he sat down with all the actors. He was very quiet, very smart. And as I sat there, in some way, I felt more free. The American movie system is very much a team effort. Everyone works with each other.

"I think that's why Arne took the chance with me. He saw something in my eyes that convinced him that I would come through. He put a strange confidence in my person, but I'm very glad he did."

— CHAPTER SIX —

The next six months passed in a blur of activity for Antonio. Despite the long hours, he was fueled by the excitement of experiencing a new life. He walked the streets of New York in wide-eyed wonder, not at the city per se, but that he was there living the chance of a lifetime.

"You know, like the song, if you can make it there, you'll make it anywhere," Banderas joked.

The physical filming of the movie was only part of Banderas's introduction to movies, American style. Once filming ended on *The Mambo Kings*, he went back home awhile, then returned to America for an even more frenzied time—he was about to be introduced to those American movie traditions, the press junket and publicity tour. In a seemingly never-ending series of interviews, even the verbose Banderas began to run out of original things to say.

He was amazed at the depth of some reporters' questions or the minutiae others waded in. He found himself shooting off answers as fast as they were asked.

"I will always make Spain my home. Even London is very different from Spain but when I'm in England at least I know I'm in Europe. I'm happier in my own land. I don't want to lose my roots. I think a man without roots is nobody."

"You must excuse me, I am a European smoker. Everyone in Europe smokes, unlike here."

"I don't like to be a star. Well, maybe for five minutes a day, but no more. As a star, you have to be brilliant all the time. I like to just act. I want to play characters. I have to be with my feet on the earth, not a butterfly. I am just Antonio."

"Hollywood is like a femme fatale. She can give you a lot but she can also strip you of everything. One must treat her with a great deal of caution, with one's feet firmly on the earth, not kicking the dust up with her."

But the whirlwind of interviews and promotion was doing a most important thing for Banderas—it was giving him name recognition. Antonio never worried about people believing he could act. Instead, he was more concerned that Americans like him. He understood that Hollywood stars were as well known for their personalities as they were for their talent. And from the beginning, he had most of the people he met falling victim to his charms. He went out of his way to make sure they would.

For example, in an article for *Mirabella*, writer Trish Deitch Rohrer could barely contain herself. Accustomed to interviewing wary celebrities who act as if they'd rather be anywhere but with a reporter, Rohrer was swept off her feet by Banderas's open-arms interview policy—not to mention his charm and looks.

"Banderas is the baby-faced heartthrob who inhabits most of Spanish director Pedro Almodovar's films, and here he is, sitting across from you in a chi-chi West Hollywood restaurant, putting the same kind of energy into the conversation that the rare man puts into an all-nighter in bed. He wipes his mouth on the edge of the tablecloth, then leans close to you and in the broken English he's learned only in the last five months, says sincerely, 'What can I done?'"

Apparently, unsure whether or not he had completely charmed the pants off this interviewer, Antonio gives her a parting shot.

"The meal is over and Banderas whispers a few words of Spanish into your tape recorder for later. Then he dutifully follows his newly arrived publicist outside and behind her back, blows you several tiny, illicit kisses before climbing into his limousine and heading back into a world where Hollywood is just another word in a language he barely understands."

Another journalist, Lynn Snowden, approached her interview with Banderas from a more cynical point of view. Unlike other journalists, Snowden does not seem impressed with Banderas's command of English, and in fact, sees Antonio's apologies for his still-imperfect use of the language as disingenuous, a calculated bit meant to wow the interviewer.

Antonio seems to sense her critical eye and goes out of his way to keep Snowden off balance by not being the person she or most Americans will initially expect him to be.

"It's madness for an interviewer to expect an actor to be like his characters, but I wasn't prepared for such a dramatic difference; the actor known for playing quiet, smoldering, nearly mute types is, in person, much more the hammy theatrical actor than the subtly played movie star.

"In a fit of laughter in the hotel lounge, he flops backward on the settee and kicks his booted feet into the air, causing a waiter to pause in midstep. In New York, walking down Broadway, he strikes extravagant poses at the street corners, loudly singing snatches of show tunes—he loves American musicals—and pop songs, even though it's pouring rain and I'm mortified. His coolness is so lacking at this point that two teenage girls passing by wonder if he's 'the guy from *Truth or Dare*' and decide that he isn't."

Determined to regain control of the interview, Snowden tries to put Antonio on the hot seat, but he deflects her attempts to pin him down about anything serious. In the end, Snowden seems piqued and frustrated with Antonio for being so different than what she expected.

"No wonder he and Madonna get along. . . . He seems determined to be outrageous. At one point, sitting in a crowded bar, he leans over and rather grotesquely licks my cheek. . . . He laughs at seeing me lose my cool and wipe my cheek."

But Snowden's horror is a minority sentiment. For the most part, Banderas made friends with his obvious willingness to open himself up as wide as his inquisitors wanted. Journalists are so used to being treated like the enemy, or most often scum, by celebrities, finding one who actually seemed eager to talk made him an immediate favorite. When asked a question, he thought about his answer and gave the impression he wasn't just rattling off prefab answers.

But it was strenuous work and by the end of an exhausting three-week promotional blitz for *The Mambo Kings*, Banderas's energy level had noticeably waned. He even tells one journalist of his anxiety about doing a television interview.

"It is much more difficult. To you, in person, I can explain something using my body. But that's not possible with television. More than that, though, I'm a little bit tired of Antonio. All the time talking about Antonio—I have had enough of Antonio, up to here."

In the end, it was a good thing Banderas worked

so hard to make himself memorable in print because *The Mambo Kings* turned out to be a huge disappointment, at least from a box office point of view. As so often happens, something was lost in the translation from written word to film. Parts of the book about sex and food that gave it such substance were pared away, leaving only the barebones story of the two brothers who emigrate to New York in the 50s.

Not that it was a critical disaster of *Ishtar* proportions. *Time* magazine's David Ansen critically praised the film's atmosphere and depth.

"Exuberant, melancholic, and sometimes narratively messy, Glimcher and screenwriter Cynthia Gore don't always cross their t's and dot their i's but in the face of such juice, who cares. There's depth and complexity to the characters in *Mambo Kings*. Destined for a moment of glory on *I Love Lucy*, they avidly participate in their own downfall, clinging stubbornly to their delusions."

And about Antonio, he offered this praise.

"Banderas had to learn English to play this role, but you wouldn't know it: he plumbs all the nuances of charm and self-pity in Nestor's melancholic soul."

Premiere's Marilyn Bathany was less concerned with characterization than about Banderas's overall love affair with the screen.

"In *The Mambo Kings*, he does things to a trumpet that had his fans fervently wishing they were made of brass. In short, Banderas has resurrected the Latin Lover from the trash heap of moldy cultural icons and given it currency—astonishing, considering the sexual squeamishness of the times.

"But then, Banderas isn't just another too-suave-by-half seduction artiste. Yes, he's seriously cute. But he's also a protean actor who can make any character, no matter how nuts, irresistible and any sex act, no matter how kinky, seem as innocent as a puppyish romp."

Antonio was also given high marks by his costar, who knows a thing or two about the Latin Lover convention.

"He's one of the most gifted actors I've ever come across, let alone worked with" Armande Assante said. "He's an amazing talent. He has the kind of sensitivity that Montgomery Clift had—vulnerable. In fact, it's an extraordinary vulnerability for a man and he's completely unashamed and unabashed about showing it."

Banderas was equally enthusiastic in his praise

of his costars, particularly Maruschka Detmers, who played his wife.

"She's very cerebral, very smart, and was all the time asking questions about the character. But more than that, she has amazing eyes and shows so much emotion in them. Something tragic, like she has some terrible torment going on inside—which she does in this movie.

"At one moment she can be as vulnerable as a baby and the next she suddenly becomes this incredible woman. She has a beautiful soul."

If the sex symbol image had been an occasional blip on Banderas's screen career in Spain, it became a glaring beacon of interest in America. While Banderas had been able to flick aside serious discussion of his heartthrob appeal in Europe, stateside journalists forced him to confront his screen appeal in earnestness. And once realizing he was backed into a corner from which he couldn't escape, Antonio has been able to consolidate his feelings on that peculiar film phenomenon.

"At the beginning, I think it helps you, being considered a sex symbol," Banderas admitted. "If you are smart enough, you're going to take advantage of it. In another way, you are cut off from characters you might want to do. You must have the time and the opportunity to show you can do something else besides a sex symbol role.

"But the truth is, I am not a sex symbol. Sometimes, when I take photographs, I have some fun with them, but every morning when I wake up, I look in the mirror and laugh. You lose perspective and objectivity after thirty-four years. You are born with a face or a body or whatever. It's nothing I work at. I consider myself a normal person in private life.

"I didn't realize I was so passionate until I came to America," he has said dryly. "In Spain I am considered very normal because in my country, people are always passionate—about soccer matches, about everything. It's just the way we are. I do normal things. I don't, what's the word? Smolder. I play tennis. I play the piano. I talk to my family. I love music, all kinds—the Beatles, Stones, Hollies, Andrew Lloyd Webber, and opera. I enjoy working out at the gym. Most of all, I like staying home.

"Am I sexy? I always want to say, 'What the hell are you talking about?' You just cannot take yourself too seriously in this business. Or in life."

At the same time, Banderas is not one who approaches life superficially. One of his favorite pastimes is to ponder his world and matters of the soul and it's this reflection that makes him truly believe we shouldn't take ourselves too seriously, that for the most part, man gives himself way too much importance. He points out that he's more likely to be reading Stephen Hawking than movie magazines and this explains a lot of his views. The question of what is "out there" occupies more than a passing thought in Antonio's mind.

"My feelings inside myself are that maybe God exists, but those are irrational thoughts, really. But you know, I am more interested in the cosmos, the Big Bang.

"If the beginning of the universe was the first of January, well then, human beings appear on Earth with about ten minutes to go before the New Year on December 31. When you realize that and think about what it really means, it makes you feel ridiculous.

"I mean, it's like a big stone over there in the middle of nothing and we are here, with the beautiful Earth—fighting each other? If someone were to watch us from another planet, we would look so ridiculous. We are microbes, little things. I like to think that—it helps put things in their proper perspective."

When you realize the man is speaking in a language he's relatively just learned, it really does boggle the mind.

But as is his way, Banderas jumps from the sublime to the silly as he recalls the time Billy Crystal called him The Sexiest Man Alive when he hosted the 1993 Oscar telecast.

"It's a joke, obviously. You can see for yourself. The camera loves certain people—and not necessarily the people who are beautiful when you see them in the street. My secret is that I've learned to use the camera after all my years as a movie actor.

"But, I do think I am a romantic person and

maybe that's not such a good thing nowadays, because people are more practical. Being a romantic is something that people have to carry with them, it can make life harder.

"I don't think there is any kind of plan in Hollywood to make me fill the empty space left by Valentino seventy years ago. I just try to have a certain logic about my career and the roles I pick.

"Being in front of the camera, the time between when somebody says 'Action!' and 'Cut!'—that's really my life, my space of freedom, my space to conquer. I love this profession. I love acting and I love telling stories."

Although *The Mambo Kings* didn't exactly make Antonio into an overnight superstar, he knew it was an acceptable start.

"Yes, it was disappointing the film didn't do better, but not every movie is a huge success. The trick is to take what's best about it and work with that. I learned a lot about making a movie in America—and more important, I also learned that I wanted to do more here. Once that decision was made, the next question was how to go about it.

"I've never minded taking smaller roles in films that intrigue me. I'd always gone anywhere to play interesting roles. But right then, Hollywood was treating me like a king and it was a wonderful experience. So I decided to push a little and see what I could make happen.

"On one hand, I do not plan things. I've never

planned my career just like I can't worry about my image. But you can be open to things in a certain way and that is what I did. I'm like a little ant, building something little by little and I hope, because of that approach, I have built a stronger structure than I would have otherwise. It's the projects themselves that intrigue me, not the size of the part they offer."

Committing himself to giving America a serious career shot meant giving up many things he'd become accustomed to.

"It was difficult, sacrificing so many things— among them top billing," Antonio has said honestly, referring to that all-important status symbol among actors. "But, it was a small price to pay for what I was hoping to gain."

— CHAPTER SEVEN —

Even though *The Mambo Kings* failed to live up to its prerelease hype, it proved to be an invaluable showcase for Banderas. It's amazing to realize that up until then, America was literally the only country in the Western world where Banderas wasn't a huge star. But finally, thanks to his soulful portrayal of Nestor, American directors began to sit up and take notice. Here was a unique specimen—a handsome movie star who could actually act as good as he looked.

There was only one little snag—that pesky language problem. Not to mention a heavy accent. But Banderas was already working feverishly to perfect his English and most directors and producers were uniformly astounded at his command of the language after so short a time.

Banderas was considered for many roles and although nothing worked out at first, he knew the importance of at least making personal contact with the Hollywood creative community. Among those he met in the months after *The Mambo Kings* were John Badham and most thrillingly for Antonio, Francis Ford Coppola. Banderas relishes the memory of meeting such a film icon.

"An agent from ICM took me to Francis's home on a Sunday morning," Antonio has said with a smile. "I thought I was going to a Beverly Hills mansion, but it's a very normal home in a very Italian style, like a villa. I rang the bell a long time and stood there waiting, thinking nobody was going to ever answer the door. What was strange is that I could hear the television inside. Just when I was sure nobody was going to answer and I would have to walk home, Francis came to the door—with a towel wrapped around his waist.

"He invited me in and asked if I wanted to watch television or if I'd like something to eat or drink. I found him very natural, very comfortable, very charming, like someone from Italy or Spain. Well, you know Francis and wine. We sat drinking some of the wine he bottles himself and had a very nice conversation about Italy and mothers, of all things. You see, it was Mother's Day and he told me that I must call my mother back in Spain. It was a very nice day, although we really didn't talk about films too much.

"A week later, Francis called me up and told me

he was going to send me some scenes from a movie he was preparing to do. He asked if I would mind reading to play *Dracula*. I said, of course I wouldn't mind.

"We made arrangements to meet in a big empty church on Hollywood Boulevard, where I spent the whole afternoon reading. It was most unique. Your footsteps make these eerie echoes and you could hear your voice bouncing off the walls.

"And Francis, he'd whisper things like, 'Very good.' But also strange things like, 'Keep a secret from me. Invent something horrible if you like, say, you killed your mother with a knife and hid her in a suitcase.' It was quite a day."

Two weeks later, Coppola called Banderas and asked him to fly up to San Francisco.

"He told me to bring my wife and that we'd spend a nice day together talking and walking around the city. And that's what we did. The boat from *Apocalypse Now* was out there. The whole thing was like a living museum. I ended up screen testing for *Dracula*, without Winona. Instead I was filmed with my wife and the whole time, Francis was eating spaghetti, talking to my wife about my performance.

" 'Look at your husband. He looks very good, doesn't he?' Things like that. Ultimately, I didn't get the part, but it was such a nice, strange experience. Like working with a god. I've sometimes thought I should write a story, *My Three Days with Francis*."

With nothing appearing immediately on the horizon, Banderas signed on to play the lead in an Italian miniseries, *Young Mussolini*. But it wasn't long before Banderas snagged two film roles. The first was an art-house adaptation of Isabel Allende's *House of the Spirits*. The movie traces the fifty-year arc of the Trueba family, from its patriarch's discovery of gold through the military coup that threatens to destroy it. Told from the perspective of the three main women characters, the novel has touched a chord with readers the world over.

In *House of the Spirits*, Banderas happily took fifth billing behind Jeremy Irons, Meryl Streep, Glenn Close and, ironically, Winona Ryder. It was a prestigious project, based on Allende's sweeping, award-winning novel. There was some personal irony for Banderas as well.

"The first movie project that ever brought me to America was *Of Love and Shadows* that I was going to make with Betty Kaplan. I had begun taking English courses but the film's financing fell through so the project was scrapped. I still hope Betty will get her film made someday.

"So, now I had come full circle, making another Allende project in English. To work with the people of the level that I did in *House of the Spirits* was a pleasure. My memories of it are all very good."

Although the book was considered by many to be a masterpiece, the same could not be said of the movie. But typically, Banderas came away unscathed. One reviewer singled him out this way.

"Though the star-heavy casting is necessary to flesh out characters that the viewer can tell are meant to be extraordinary and compelling, only Banderas really registers. Meryl Streep, Glenn Close, and Jeremy Irons are fine, if physically miscast. Ryder once again proves she is Keanu Reeves with breasts.

"What could have been another stock character for Banderas as a fiery Latin activist, is—once again—made so much more by the sheer force of his own undeniable star power."

Banderas knew the movie had bitten off more than it could chew but he still thought the final product was worthwhile.

"In some ways, it is very much a film about women and what they teach men," Antonio explained. "It examined the interaction between men and women and the love they share.

"Most films are made by men for young boys. This was a beautiful experience because it was fresh. My character in the movie is not a big character and there is not enough time, probably, to get the whole feeling of him. I was struggling to bring him alive. But when I saw the movie for the first time, I was proud to be part of it because it is not usual.

"In many ways, 'the everything' in the movie is told from the point of view of women. That's what is wonderful for me. There's a lot of sensitivity and spirituality. And, of course, because it's a movie talking about freedom, talking about an era in South America where the people were very conscious of political events, the dictatorships."

Banderas says that he personalized some of the movie because of his own country's struggles under Franco and the cost of living under his regime.

"Every dictatorship is different, of course, due to the features of the country, but in some ways I was reminded of Spain's past. I was very young when Franco died. I only realized what it had been like to live under Franco three or four years after he died, because the country just exploded then, just flowered."

While most moviegoers forgot about *The House of the Spirits* quickly, it was a role that stayed with Banderas for a while. In fact, Banderas got so wrapped up in his ill-fated romance with Winona Ryder's character, he says he needed a couple of weeks to get over the emotion of it all.

"It was hard to say good-bye to those characters. I really thought a lot about what happened to them all. I cared a lot about Winona's character. Partly because when you held Winona, she seemed so fragile it felt as if she would break. I became very protective."

The other film role Banderas landed had serious career implications. Not only was it a big-budget Hollywood movie, it was already generating heat as "the" controversial film of the year. *Philadelphia*, starring Tom Hanks, would be the first major Hollywood motion picture to deal with AIDS. Banderas, who had played gay characters almost as often as heterosexual ones, jumped at the chance. This was his moment of truth, he just knew it.

Directed by Jonathan Demme, fresh off his Oscar win for *Silence of the Lambs*, *Philadelphia* told the story of an AIDS-stricken attorney who sues his law firm for discrimination when they fire him after learning of his illness. Hanks was hired to play the sympathetic attorney, with Banderas aboard as his fiercely loyal lover, Miguel Alvarez.

Although it shouldn't have been unexpected, Antonio was surprised by the amount of concern it caused people that he was willing to portray gay characters. When one journalist worried that Banderas might be jeopardizing his career by accepting the role in *Philadelphia* after the homosexual leanings of some of his other film characters, Antonio's answer was abrupt.

"If a director is not going to call me because I take a role as a gay, then I am not proud to be part of this profession," he said, dismissing the danger of being typecast. "The role was a little dangerous, but not so difficult. I think *Philadelphia* is very hopeful and audiences can see that this is a movie about love. The film is very much from the heart. To the heart. I feel proud to be involved in a movie like this. For me, it is more than a movie. It's something else. It's an interesting voyage.

"I am completely proud to play a gay character. People think it's going to create a polemic and a controversy. I just do not understand that. It would make me crazy if I thought every movie I made had to be a step forward in my career. If I have to worry that someone doesn't want to work with me because I've played someone gay, well, that's pretty sad.

"But it would have been surprising for me if the producers and actors said to me, 'Hey, Antonio, we cannot count on you because the image you have in the public eye is that you are homosexual.' Like I say, I would not be proud of my profession if someone says those kinds of stupid things."

Despite being born and raised in a mostly Catholic country, Banderas swears there is much less homophobia in Spain than he now understands exists in America.

"Homosexuality is much more accepted there than it is here in America. It is absurd. I am an actor. I am not playing at this, like in high school or college. I am a professional and I do the roles as honestly as I can. Plus. You must realize because of the social difficulties, gay roles often have a lot of inherent drama, which is good for an actor to do."

And as such, while it was nothing for an actor to play gay characters as Banderas did in Europe, he suddenly realized some people saw it as career suicide this side of the Atlantic. It's always an interesting part of Hollywood lore the number of actors who shy away from gay roles, whether out of concern for their image—or because it may hit a little too close to home.

"Maybe that's why I was chosen for the role. I did gay roles before and producers and directors probably think that I don't have any problems playing a gay character—and they are right. I am not going to behave differently in front of people because I am playing a gay character. I don't have to go around with gays to see what they do.

"I don't like to talk about the differences between gays and straights—it's like talking about the differences between men and women. I don't see differences that way. To me, my character in *Philadelphia*, Miguel, is probably just like me, except we have a different sexuality."

At the same time, Banderas has said he never had the intention of being known specifically for his gay roles.

"Look, if I play five gay characters, I am going to say no to the sixth. It is not because I have anything against gays or because I am scared. It is just the same as if I played five policemen in a row, I am going to grow tired of playing the same character again and again. All actors need variety to keep fresh. But roles should be picked for what they have to offer and not run from out of fear you may offend some sensibilities.''

From the inception of the film, director Demme knew the part of Miguel was crucial.

''Everyone understood that the place where we were either going to win people over or lose them totally was with the relationship between Hanks's character and his lover,'' Demme has said bluntly.

''If we wanted the audience to accept Tom Hanks as gay and root for him as a hero, then it was imperative that the audience also support and root for his relationship. We had to find someone who would be perceived as a wonderful boyfriend. That was the big question—who were we going to find to play Miguel who could pull his weight opposite Tom as an actor and at the same time play well with a straight audience?

''Antonio was a godsend because his appeal cuts right across all sexual preferences, I think. And I think it's because he's so centered as a human being. I knew women would adore seeing him. I was confident gay males would adore seeing him. And I was even confident that he was a cool enough guy that straight males would understand his appeal without feeling threatened by it.''

Even All-American boy Hanks understood Banderas's same-sex appeal.

"I wasn't kidding what I said at the Oscars, if things were different for me, I'd go after Antonio like a shot, that he'd be the only person I'd leave my wife for," Tom has said. "The first day we were on the set shooting, Antonio is there in those tight pants, wearing that cute leather jacket and I thought, 'You know, if I were gay, I'd flip over this guy. I'd be nuts about him.' It was a funny realization. It's just the whole package—he's dark, he is mysterious and yet he is so full of zest for living and completely accepting in that wise, old world way.

"When the movie came out, I got a kick knowing I was the envy of ninety-five percent of the women in the world—and I guess about seventeen percent of the men. Antonio would be an easy man for anyone to love."

And love is ultimately what Banderas says is the point of the whole movie.

"Miguel loves Andy so much. Miguel's the one who is going to live, who's going to keep the pain forever. He sacrifices a lot to be together—he is face to face with death. He wants to fight, even with his hands, against the disease, but he can't. He's keeping all the energy inside himself until he's ready to explode.

"In the last scene they find a mystical and peaceful way to say good-bye to each other. You can see they are going to share everything, even death, and accept it. That's why Miguel slowly kisses each of his lover's fingers as he is passing to the other side."

The fact that Banderas is able to reduce the most controversial of relationships into the basic human conditions is the secret of his acting strength. Ultimately, he seeks to talk to the human in each of us—and respects his characters as people regardless of their particular situation.

"It is true, I am very respectful of my work," Antonio agreed. "At the same time, I don't believe in people without a sense of humor. Being able to find the humorous side of a situation, any situation, is the sign of true intelligence."

Banderas has hit his appeal—and his ability to make palatable the most uncommon characters—on the head. It's his unique combination of smarts, humor, and talent that sets him apart among actors anywhere. And Antonio is as good as an audience member as he is a performer. Not only does he exude intelligence and humor, he appreciates it in others. Despite the heavy subject matter of *Philadelphia* Banderas and Demme's lighthearted outlook kept the set relaxed and comfortable.

"Jonathan Demme has got to be the funniest man on earth," Banderas enthused. "I was not at all surprised when he told me how *Law of Desire* is one of his favorite Almodovar films. I told him that he must have come from the underground cinema because he's just too crazy.

"One time we shot a Halloween party scene and

Jonathan came dressed, and shot the scenes, in a flowery shirt, Bermuda shorts, sunglasses and a big camera and Hawaiian lei hanging from his neck. There was never any tension on the set at all. And I loved the way he used the camera. He'd do shots the way they usually show a bad guy in a terror movie walking through a hallway, looking for someone to kill, but in this case the killer is a disease.

"Jonathan shoots so many different ways, you can't figure out how he's going to edit it all together. For example, there was one scene where I come to the hospital and we first shot it in a traditional way. My take, then Tom's take. Then he had me talk directly to the camera, as if it were Tom in the hospital bed. I even had to put my hand on the camera, saying, 'Oh, you've got a fever, baby?'

"I suspect Jonathan did that so he would have an option in editing."

Banderas hasn't spent this many years in film for nothing. Demme indeed was giving himself plenty of leeway and in the end, chose the safest route possible for portraying Miguel—that is, as antiseptically as possible. Much of the intimate scene between Banderas and Hanks was left on the cutting-room floor out of concern that the American public wasn't ready to see its movie stars portraying that side of a gay man. Sick and dying and underdog, sure. Sexual, no.

Newsweek's David Ansen, for one, felt Demme should have been braver and trusted people to accept Banderas more.

> "Though their brief scenes convey both the tenderness and the irritations of a longtime intimacy, the movie owes us more than this truncated glimpse into our hero's personal life."

If Banderas feels he was shortchanged in the final cut, he refuses to say so. He is nothing if not professional. And from a career perspective, he had made a giant step forward, starring in a commercially successful Hollywood picture with the eventual Oscar winner. If the roles ended up smaller, fine, as long as there was progression. Beyond his personal advancement, Banderas feels passionately that he was involved with something worthwhile as a human being—spreading the message of tolerance.

"Now that Tom Hanks has played a gay man, maybe next time around, there will be that much less worry. I do believe stuff is changing. Look at the work Elizabeth Taylor has dome for AIDS awareness. Look at the quality of actor who participated in *Philadelphia*—Denzel Washington, Joanne Woodward, Mary Steenburgen, and Jason Robards. They all wanted to be in an entertaining movie, but one that was important, too. None of them had second thoughts. It was so important then, and still is, to send this message about AIDS everywhere."

And it's a message that is very personal to Banderas. Like anyone in the arts, Antonio has been touched by AIDS as it brutally ravages the international artistic community. Although he is usually untiringly upbeat off-camera, AIDS is one subject that has made him pause in melancholy—out of respect as much as sadness.

"I have lost friends, very close friends of mine, to this disease. I know many people who have died and who are suffering the sickness now. You know, I remember the last day we were on the set and a crew member who had AIDS came up to say good-bye. And I said, 'I'll see you at the premiere.' And he said. 'If I'm still alive.' And it caused me this pain," Antonio clutched his chest.

"He didn't say it feeling sorry for himself. It was just his fact of life. And it hurt because the truth was, I didn't know if I would see him there.

"If in fifteen years we look back and realize we've done nothing, and by that I mean no paintings, no movies, no plays about what is happening here with this disease, then we will not be able to say we are artists.

"All the experiences that I had in the movie are inside of me and this is going to make me richer in reflections. I am proud to be part of a project that talks about something that is going on in our society, and I hope it makes people understand all the suffering."

— CHAPTER EIGHT —

After his initial struggles with English, Banderas has said a curious thing happened around the time he began working on his next two films, *Miami Rhapsody* and *Interview With the Vampire*.

"I suddenly had the sense of this great freedom working in a foreign language. When I say, in Spanish, 'I love you,' I know the value of the words. But when I speak in English, I feel freer to jump into lines like that with more abandon, and less preconceived baggage. If you are *too* conscious of what you're doing and saying every single moment, then something loses its freshness.

"Plus, I actually began dreaming in English. Someone once told me that a good way to learn a new language was to try and dream in it. I don't know about that, but I was surprised when I realized I was suddenly hearing English in my sleep."

Although he was still restricted by his accent, Banderas found ever more doors opening for him. In fact, it was more like floodgates. In 1994, Banderas's movies were everywhere as Antonio was earning a reputation as an actor who could do almost anything. His latest casting coup was signing on with another hot property, *Interview With the Vampire.*

"I am a very big fan of Anne Rice so I signed up to play Armand even though I wasn't sure whether Daniel Day Lewis, Jeremy Irons, or whoever might play Lestat," Banderas has said. "The script is strange and touching and the project has such a long history, years and years. I was most curious to see what Neil Jordan would do with this piece, especially after *The Crying Game*," he has explained, referring to the film's director.

"I was getting to play a five-hundred-year-old vampire. There was terror, yes, but it was romantic and sexy, too. It was going to be very wild. They were letting me fly and beat people up and eat people. I couldn't wait to get started because it was going to be very nice."

As you may have gathered, Armand, the ancient leader of the Theatre des Vampires in Paris, where vampires pretend to be actors pretending to be vampires for the titillation of the audience, is one of the film's more flamboyant blood-suckers. And—surprise—was once one of Lestat's male lovers. A couple hundred years or so earlier.

"Yes, he's a gay character," Antonio sighed in one interview, as if a great weight had just been dumped on his weary chest. Then he brightened. "But since there is no sex between vampires, it's kind of strange to call him gay, don't you think? Since he's hundreds of years old, he's many, many other things, too."

Director Jordan knew he had a surefire audience pleaser in Banderas, who was almost too enthusiastic to play the role of the undead—his eyes seemed to glisten a little too happily when planning scenes of neck biting and bloodletting. Jordan wanted to emphasize the powerfully primitive, primal aspect of being a vampire, so he dressed Antonio in red velvet and had him wear his hair long.

"I felt at that point the story needed Antonio's thunderous sexual presence. He can make theatricality work in a movie—which a lot of actors can't."

Because people so often get stuck on his looks, it's easy to forget that Banderas is an immensely gifted actor, and that at the end of the day, talent has a way of smoothing a lot of rough edges.

"Some people get their English down, but they lose their heart," is the way *Interview With the Vampire* casting agent Juliet Taylor put it. "For some reason, many performers are never able to convey their essential great quality in English. Antonio, however, does not have that problem."

Not everyone had such faith, however, in Banderas's costar, Tom Cruise. As soon as his casting was announced, fans of the book nearly stormed the studio. Even Anne Rice squirted fuel on the controversy by publicly expressing doubt over Cruise's ability to effectively portray her beloved vampire. That doubt later gave way to lavish praise after Rice saw the performance.

Banderas felt bad for Cruise, who he feels is a likable guy who tries hard to better his craft.

"A lot of people complained about the casting of Tom Cruise but I always thought Tom was a brilliant actor," Antonio has said charitably. "He's an incredible worker. I said all along that people were going to be surprised and that the controversy would end when the movie came out.

"It was understandable why people got so upset. It was a very popular book and everyone had their own idea for it. They didn't want their imaginations violated by the movie. The bottom line is, they will either pay their money and see the movie or not. People always have to remember, though, that cinema and literature are completely different. But those who came with an open mind were surprised, I think, in a positive way."

Although critics of Cruise tended to skirt the issue, the biggest problem with Cruise as Lestat at the end of the day wasn't his acting ability or even the sexuality of the role. Where Cruise fell short was his inhibition. He's simply not an actor comfortable being brazenly sensual onscreen. Probably because he's not terribly sensual offscreen. He truly is the All-American, white-bread boy next door. In person, he doesn't exude a lustily passionate personality. *Erotic* is not a typical adjective used when describing Cruise.

Then there's our hero. Casting Banderas caused only delight among fans of the book and moviegoers in general. And it was no great surprise that he generated the best reviews and reactions. One reviewer recounted an experience at a screening.

"The opening credits rolled at an early Hollywood screening of *Interview With the Vampire*. A polite smattering of applause for Tom Cruise, along with a few hisses. Hearty cheers and wolf whistles for Brad Pitt. Then the name Antonio Banderas flashed on the wide screen: Pandemonium. And the performance was there to back it up.

"Playing Anne Rice's imperious Armand, the world's oldest living vampire, Banderas transmitted the depths of the character's melancholia and frustration with his expressive eyes. The reaction of the *New York Daily News*'s Jami Bernard was typical—she ended her review by offering Banderas her own neck to bite."

Newsweek did their own biting.

"Pitt's at his best in the present-day scenes. Cruise works hard to affect a haughty, supercilious manner, and he's not bad, but you sense both these men are struggling to find a style any number of classically trained actors could pull off in their sleep."

Not surprisingly, the one classically trained actor in the group is the one who stands out in the film, able to navigate the film's heightened drama and focus it at a cinematic level.

"But Antonio Banderas is a commanding Armand."

For all the critical brouhaha, *Interview With the Vampire* was a box office success and therefore another positive notch on Banderas's Hollywood belt. In film lingo, there was a lot of buzz on Banderas, he was generating a lot of heat in both theaters and boardrooms. For his part, Antonio just kept working.

Banderas's plan was working masterfully, and his agent, Nunez, has nurtured his career and price tag with utmost care, like a chess game.

"We used *Philadelphia* to get him *Interview With the Vampire*," said the agent. "Then we used *Vampire* to increase his asking price."

Which is now estimated to be in the four million dollars per picture range. But it's clear that quality has always mattered more to Banderas.

"I will work for free if I think the project is valuable" he has said, meaning it. "However, I'm not stupid. If they are going to pay me handsomely, I'm not going to refuse it. There is a business reality here—one day everyone can want you for their picture, then if you have a few bad movies in a row, nobody wants to hire you. You need to put away for when you have to go back and work in the theater for nothing."

Miami Rhapsody, considered a "little picture," offered Banderas a chance to loosen up a bit, playing a charming Cuban émigré who romantically services three generations of Miami women, including Mia Farrow and Sarah Jessica Parker.

The film's writer and director, David Frankel, decided to create the part for him after watching Madonna threaten to soak her head in the toilet after Banderas shows up with his wife in *Truth or Dare*.

"It was just great, someone who could make Madonna react that way," Frankel has said. "And he seemed to take it all in stride."

But more than that, Frankel recognized Banderas's ability to play to both men and women.

"Men and women like him equally because he doesn't have that macho baggage," Frankel has explained. "He doesn't alienate the guys in the audience, even though their girlfriends are sitting their fantasizing their little hearts out. He's just got this duality that lets him get away with things.

"For example, who else on earth can play a rapist and a kidnapper and not only make him palatable—but likable?"

But Frankel also noticed something else about Banderas, an interesting duality.

"The first time I had lunch with Antonio, I knew it was very important to him to become a star. And he's worked very hard at achieving that end."

"Maybe I am ambitious," Banderas has allowed. "But it's about the work. I want to be able to do all of these projects, I want to do all sorts of different parts and it's easier to get that chance if you are considered a star."

Alex Keshishian, who directed *Truth or Dare*, has said Antonio's cross-appeal opened a lot of doors for him, even before he was a well-known name.

"He seems to get away with being traditionally macho and yet remarkably gentle at the same time. It's interesting that people have compared him to Valentino because there *is* a magic quality to his face that is as pure as a silent-film star's. It can convey a lot of emotion—or allow an audience to project a lot of emotion onto it."

Not only was Banderas a hit with the people he worked with and the mainstream press, alternative journalists like *The Village Voice*'s Michael Musto were drooling over Antonio. Banderas spent time with the flamboyant Musto at a screening of *Miami Rhapsody* at the Miami Film Festival. Ironically, Banderas was back in Miami shooting *Two Much*, the movie that would change his life in ways unimaginable. Musto recounts the experience with a typically funny column from the writer.

"I can't seem to get into the damned New York Film Festival," grouses Musto, "but I'd rather go to Miami's anyway. It's smoothly run against a paradisiacal setting, with a diversity of films and a variety of buffets. True, you can't even eat a burger on Ocean Drive without someone stepping in to mousse and style your hair but at least you can then return to the movie theater feeling not only welcome, but sated and well-groomed.

"*Miami Rhapsody* itself feels glib and entertaining and derivative, the only thing that separates it from a Woody imitation being the two black characters (one of them is Naomi Campbell stretching as a narcissistic model). Still, the locations alone got cheers and Antonio Banderas is expectedly irresistible as Antonio, the bongo-playing nurse.

"And he's hot in person too, wouldn't you know. . . . And he's a star still willing to play tons and tons of gay characters, thank heavens.

" 'I don't have any problems with homosexuals,' he said, 'and I'm not going to have problems to play them in the future. I'm not playing homosexuals being a queen. I play a guy like me. It's not so far from what I am.'

"Hmm. *Now* we were getting warmer. When he played gay men in Almodovar flicks, Banderas noted, people really *believed* he was gay.

" 'I said, what does this prove? That I'm a good actor!' "

Antonio's life was taking on that if-it's-November-I-must-be-in-Miami quality to it as he went directly from *Interview With the Vampire* into *Miami Rhapsody* with barely a noticeable break in between. But he refused to let the pace interfere with his enjoyment of knowing his career was running on all cylinders. Plus, once he arrived for work, his natural *joie de vivre* would kick in. He loved working and he loved meeting new people. Shyness was not a problem.

While Banderas's reputation as a solid actor preceded him, his co-workers were usually a little less prepared for the jubilant personality that came along with the talent. It was unusual to find a serious actor who was anything but serious once the cameras stopped rolling.

Banderas has admitted the image of him many in Hollywood first had came mostly from the broody, moody, *quiet*, characters. None of which describes the living, breathing Banderas when he walks into, and takes over, a room.

"But you know, I'm not always this quiet guy," Antonio laughed. "Nor am I always happy-go-lucky, either. I sometimes have very bad reactions to things and can have a very short temper. Later, I always regret it, but . . . You know, a doctor in Spain who was examining me put his fingers on my back and it left a mark for hours. He said to me, 'Wow, that shows that you have a temper.' "

But in a town where tantrums are often the norm, a healthy temper is readily accepted. Especially when it is balanced by an ingratiating charm.

"He's quite silly," Sarah Jessica Parker, his *Miami Rhapsody* co-star, has said. "That was really surprising. And God, he loved to sing these show tunes from *Evita*."

Banderas, who was still reliving the thrill of having been a vampire, would come to the set with pictures of himself as Armand, dressed in full red velvet and long locks. He would proudly show them to Parker, saying, 'You don't even recognize me, do you?'

"You know, every day he would teach me a new phrase in Spanish but the one I used the most often was '*Antonio es pura boca*'—Antonio is all talk," Parker has said warmly. "His deepest instinct is to flirt, to charm."

But in a good way, she added. It pleased Banderas that Parker understands he's just out to enjoy life and to try and make people he's working with enjoy the time they spend with him.

"I am moving myself through life with a sense of humor. To me, any other way is ridiculous, disgusting. You see, I never came to America looking for anything. I'm here because someone sent me a good script. If somebody calls me from India with a good script, that's where I'm going to be. I would die to work with David Lynch, with Francis Coppola, but if I'm not what people are looking for, I'll go home where I have my own work.''

Banderas had also become aware of the very different status movie stars have in America, and their unique vulnerability in a country where the Wild West mentality has yet to evolve.

''Spain is not so dangerous as it is here. In America, everyone has guns,'' Banderas has said in bemused wonderment. ''When we were making *Philadelphia*, it was almost impossible for the actors I was working with just to have a normal night in a restaurant. At least, not without bodyguards. That is no way to live.

''I'm just a happy guy. I am just like the waves on the seas, rolling in the wind. In my work, I am looking to be much better, to increase my involvement in movies, in art. I'm in love with the camera, what can I tell you?

''I don't want a big limousine. I don't care about making a lot of money. The big difference between a star and an actor is someone who knows the technique, who knows how to learn from everything that happens to him. A star is acting *himself* all the time. You have to have the energy for that and a nice character. I don't know if I'm that brilliant the whole day. I have my own shit with me all the time and I don't want to lose that. I can't have this big beautiful smile on my face all day, faking that I'm someone else, because that's insane.''

But as far as critics and audiences were con-

ANTONIO BANDERAS

cerned, Antonio could be whatever he wanted. Even when projects fell short of expectations, as had been the case with *The House of the Spirits* and would be the case with *Miami Rhapsody*, Banderas somehow always walked away without a scratch. He had now become bad-movie proof—a Teflon movie star.

In one of the kinder reviews of *Miami Rhapsody*, Antonio was held out as the one beacon of salvation.

"These characters seem to have emerged from a diminished gene pool—that is, from a bad sitcom. Banderas . . . is the only grown-up among them."

It was 1994 and Banderas was suddenly struck by the realization that, for all intents and purposes, he'd been away from Spain for a full year. He also admitted to himself that the nonstop pace was finally getting to him. Even he had limits and his weariness is evident from an interview from that time.

"I'm totally exhausted. There has been a lot of tension. I've been working very hard and so much traveling. Argentina for *Love and Shadows*; Lisbon, Portugal, and Copenhagen for *House of Spirits*; New Orleans, London, and Paris for *Interview*.

"Living in hotels isn't easy and I miss my family terribly. Sometimes before I'm leaving my home in Madrid to go on another location, I think, 'Oh, my God, I can't go.' I have to be careful not to burn

myself up. Too much work steals your soul away.
I need to refill it now."

But from a professional standpoint, the two years
of near constant work had paid off beyond Antonio's wildest dreams. The bottom line was, just as
Banderas had won over the hearts of movie fans,
he'd also won over the Hollywood community itself and by 1994 was one of the busiest actors working in America with movie commitments stretching
out a couple years in front of him. It was an em-
barrassment of riches—his plate was full to the
point of cracking.

But for all the satisfaction he felt at being accepted, Antonio wanted to make it clear he wasn't
an expatriate. He wasn't taking on an American
career only to relinquish his career in Europe.

"I would like to make a bridge between Spain
and here," Banderas mused. "I can do Spanish,
French, Mexican, or even Puerto Rican parts. The
only thing I'm probably never going to play is the
role of a guy from Oklahoma or Wyoming."

Not that he might not want to try. His appreci-
ation of all things American—as opposed to the
snobbery often expressed by many Europeans actors, particularly the British—was endearing and
genuine.

"One of the things I love most about working
with Americans is their sense of humor and their
unique ability to laugh at themselves," Antonio has
said. "Not all countries are like that—they take

Antonio and brother Francisco with an older cousin. (© *Ramey Photo Agency*)

Antonio and Francisco. (© *Ramey Photo Agency*)

With mom Ana.
(© *Ramey Photo Agency*)

Photo from one of Antonio's early play productions.
(© *Ramey Photo Agency*)

The hospital where Antonio was born in Málaga.
(© *Ramey Photo Agency*)

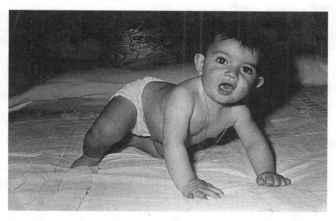

Baby Antonio. (© *Ramey Photo Agency*)

With Melanie Griffith.
(© *Ramey Photo Agency*)

Shopping. (© *Ramey Photo Agency*)

At an awards cere-
mony (photograph-
er who took this shot
does not remember
who the older gen-
tleman is). (© *Ramey
Photo Agency*)

Antonio and Melanie on the set of *Two Much*.
(© *Ramey Photo Agency*)

On the set of
Assassins.
(© *Ramey
Photo Agency*)

Photo from Antonio
and Melanie's first
public date at the
Blockbuster Awards
in Los Angeles. (©
Ramey Photo Agency)

Antonio with ex-wife Ana Leza. (© *Ramey Photo Agency*)

Antonio and Melanie on vacation in the Caribbean.
(© *Ramey Photo Agency*)

Antonio at a movie premiere. (© *Ramey Photo Agency*)

themselves too seriously. But Americans like to laugh at things, including themselves. It's very refreshing and appealing. It's what makes Americans so American.

"Americans have an incredible capacity for show business. They are very natural in front of the camera. They don't seem to be acting. They are living their characters and that's quite amazing.

"I remember once when I was working with Tom Hanks in *Philadelphia,* we were in rehearsal and just before we started shooting on the set, he was talking to me in character. Suddenly I said to him, 'Sorry, Tom, what did you say?' Because I thought he was talking to me, Antonio Banderas. But he wasn't, he was talking to Miguel, the character I played. He was so natural, I couldn't tell the difference between Tom the person and the character he was playing. These kind of things happen in film all the time with Americans.

"Probably for me, this is the best thing about Hollywood—how wonderful the actors are. It was kind of surprising because a lot of people back home warned me before I came here, 'Oh, Hollywood. That's a jungle, man. I was expecting all the time to find the lion in the jungle, but so far I haven't."

The press notwithstanding.

Banderas is candidly blunt about the other big draw of working in Hollywood—the money. Both his own personal paycheck and the amount available to pour into projects. For someone who started out in underground films not knowing if there was money to shoot the next day, the luxury of doing a project the monied way is a great comfort.

"Directors here want to know if I'm malleable," Banderas has said of the good relationship he has with directors. "I don't go to auditions putting on a character like a new skin. I just try to understand what the director wants of me."

Is it that Antonio is the true exception to the rule, an actor whose combination of vitality, good looks, and talent have allowed him to shatter the foreign actor barrier—a barrier that will magically reassemble as soon as he's passed through, blocking the way of others wanting to follow him in?

He's in rarefied company, joining the likes of Arnold Schwarzenegger, Marlene Dietrich, or Ingrid Bergman to be on the brink of A-list superstardom. Many European actors have found homes in American films, including Gerard Depardieu, Jean-Claude Van Damme, and one of the brightest young shining stars, Juliette Binoche.

But Antonio is fighting the stereotype of the Latin Lover as much as he's battling his accent. It's not just that he's foreign-born, it's that he's a *Spanish* heartthrob. Schwarzenegger got his foot in the door as an action-adventure hero, ditto Van Damme. Those are characters of few words and over-the-top actions. Antonio, however, is trying to find success right where Americans live, as the romantic leading man, with an occasional dangerous edge.

That's why people in the know in the U.S. film industry were so amazed Banderas was so willing to take on very un-leading man gay roles. But he was an actor with a method to his madness—you have to get your foot in the door before you can come in and redecorate the room.

Typically, Banderas shies away from suggestions that it's his own personal force of nature that's allowed him to accomplish what others across the seas have only dreamed. Instead, he credits the openness of an increasingly informed world.

"The world has shrunk," Banderas has said simply. "Cultural barriers have diminished so audiences accept a more foreign flavor in American films."

Maybe so, but it does ring slightly untrue, because Banderas's career in Hollywood didn't happen by chance or an act of God. It was the result of a clearly defined choice to go for it, and a carefully designed plan to take higher-profile small roles that would get him noticed.

Ultimately, it netted him a new country of adoring fans, a hot streak of landing films not seen since Michael Caine seemed to appear in every other film in the 80s, and the respect of an industry he revered.

In the long run, though, his career achievements may ultimately be of secondary importance to Antonio. Because what stands out more is the havoc his success wreaked on his personal life, resulting in the casualty of his marriage. And that, in the end, may prove to be the most lasting legacy of Hollywood.

— CHAPTER NINE —

B anderas was approaching the point of no return, both professionally and personally. Much
of the unrestrained, unbridled enthusiasm apparent in early interviews was gone by the time 1994
was nearing an end. In its place was a more
thoughtful, even pensive, mood. It seems obvious
that Antonio sensed some major changes were
coming. But would the dawn bring sunshine or
dark clouds?

"Hollywood isn't reality," Banderas once mused.
"In Hollywood we are creating lies, we are creating
stories. We are professional liars. I'm not criticizing
the system. Movies can be used in many ways. Just
look at the movies that get nominated each year for
Best Picture, like *Schindler's List*. These movies do
a great job and many of them, like a *Schindler's List*,
is an example of what movies can do for people

around the world. You know, in Europe, the new fascists are becoming huge again. Especially in Germany. But this movie showed people how it was and what is the color and the face of horror."

Banderas then shifts gears, because the real lies he's talking about are of a more personal nature, like the ones we tell ourselves.

"I think the trick here is to be smart enough not to be captured by The Industry. The candy is so big that you want to eat it, the whole thing, the first day you arrive. But I am not that way. I prefer to take my career step by step. I don't want to be in a hurry, I want to be with my feet on the ground, knowing who I am.

"I am a very lucky man but I don't want to become crazy about Hollywood. I think Hollywood can use me, I can use Hollywood and it's the perfect time for us."

The more his career took off in America, the further and further Banderas drifted from the life he had built in Spain. And that included his wife, Ana. Suddenly after so many years together, after she had been at his side through all his career successes, he felt her slipping away. Or more accurately, felt them slipping away from each other.

In a November 1994 interview, Antonio puts on his best face regarding their relationship and the ties that were still binding them.

"She's excited and happy about my career, but it is harder than before because we are traveling all the time, living in hotels. We don't have children yet, but yeah, yeah I want them!

"But, I don't want us to bring children into the world if we're not prepared for it. Right now, I am all over the place doing movies, over here, over there. I don't want to be traveling and shuttling them around on planes all the time. They deserve better than that.

"Plus, if we had children now, Ana is going to be tied to the children back home in Spain and it's going to interfere with her career. So, before we have children, we really have to think about the consequences. But we are young yet and have time.

"Eventually, though, I would like to have two, one our blood, and then I would like to adopt a kid. There are so many children in the world who have nothing. Ana and I recently went to Somalia with UNICEF and it was heartbreaking. They have very little food. They are naked. They sleep under the sun and the moon. I want to do something to help, even if it's just a grain of sand."

But there was much more that Banderas didn't say, like how their relationship seemed to be dissolving, bit by bit, day after day; how they couldn't talk to each other the way they once had; how they seemed to be different people from the couple who were once so in love.

In the beginning of his American adventure, Ana would travel with Antonio everywhere. But as one project spilled immediately over into another,

Ana's enthusiasm for hopscotching the world fizzled. And she was not enamored of America they way Antonio was—she didn't get the appeal. So more and more often than not, she left Antonio to his own devices. Was she testing the fates—or was it simply a symptom of her own winter of discontent? Antonio wasn't sure and offered only the lamest of excuses.

"Maybe she's trying to make a career in another way."

Banderas also noticed within himself a sudden, curious ambivalence about going back to Spain. It had been slowly creeping up on him, but he developed an unsettled agitation about being home.

"It's a strange thing." He shrugged. "I do miss many things about my country. I miss the food, the music, my family, I even miss the accent of my people. I miss the Mediterranean, the culture, things like that. When you are away for too long, you get a kid of sadness. This nostalgia is the kind you like, though. I'm a very nostalgic person. I like to think about the past—but not to *rethink* the past. I like to think in the present. But I use my past, the good things, to be someone.

"Nobody is anything without his roots. That's why I *have* to go back there for a while every year— to see my people and to see my family. To be fulfilled and have no anomie.

"But you know, when I am in Spain for more than six months now, I have to get out of my country because my spirit gets down. I like to travel and I have learned to be alone. Sometimes I have long periods of living in hotel rooms, reading and watching television, in Argentina or wherever I am.

"Whenever I am away working, I miss home so of course, when I get to Spain, for about the first fifteen days it's crazy. I just love to be there but then suddenly, after a couple of months, I start to want to go away again. I have to be around the world all the time just traveling, meeting and getting to know people.

"You know, the big ritual, the ceremony of this profession is like love. You start doing a movie, which is like a little life, you learn how to have relationships with the people in the movie, and you are putting the best energy that you have out there. And everybody else is doing the same thing. Some days you are fighting, some days you are loving each other. At the end, it's the same thing. When you are more involved with the people you have to cut that relationship, sever those ties, and everybody spreads out again. And then you have to repeat that ritual all over again.

"That's my life. I've done it forty-three times and I still love it. But going home isn't the same as it used to be."

That an actor only thirty-five years old has done forty-three films in this modern day of selective production and diminished output is an amazing feat, and a testament to his bankability. To put it in perspective, Meryl Streep has done twenty-two movies, Tom Cruise just seventeen and Brad Pitt only thirteen. Even Banderas acknowledges his prodigious productivity.

"I may never win an Oscar, but I'll end up in the *Guinnes Book of World Records*," he has joked.

But as is true with most "workaholics," delving into the job at hand was a practical way of dealing with unsettling troubles at home. Like many in a floundering marriage, Antonio hoped the rough spot would eventually smooth out on its own accord. He and Ana had been married since they were kids and things had always worked out before. As soon as things let up workwise, they'd have a chance to sit down and figure everything out.

The only question was, what break?

Antonio was being buried under work. Next in line to be released was *Desperado*, the sequel to Robert Rodriguez's low-budget hit *El Mariachi*, which had been made for seven thousand dollars in 1991. For the new movie, Rodriguez was given a six- to seven-million-dollar budget, which was still small considering all the explosive special effects in the bang-em-up film.

It was a big break for Banderas. It gave him a chance to prove his movie "legs"—could he open a movie on his name value alone? Would ticket buyers come to see him carry a movie? Antonio was about to find out. There was a lot at stake, although as usual, Banderas tried to downplay the importance of the situation.

"I suppose you could call it a big-budget movie but any movie would have a bigger budget than *El Mariachi*. When someone told me he made that film for only seven thousand dollars I was amazed. I thought, 'That's less than what my car cost.' But I tell you, I got the same level of entertainment from that movie as from movies that cost one hundred million dollars.

"It was obvious Robert Rodriguez was a really talented guy—he can make movies and is a good filmmaker. I decided I would like to know him. So a couple of days later we had lunch together. We talked a lot and got along very well. At first, he offered me the part of Bucho, the character of the brother, and gave me the script to read.

"Then a couple of weeks later, Robert called me and said, 'Forget about Bucho—do you want to do the leading character?' Naturally, I said yes."

Rodriguez had seen Banderas in *Tie Me Up! Tie Me Down!* and was blown away by his "out there" performance. Here was an actor he could work with.

"What amazed me about him was the way he moves," Rodriguez has said. "He has that strong Latin energy and he can summon up this very physical, visceral force that doesn't look fake. That's why we didn't use a stunt double for him—

because he doesn't move like a clunky American. When he moves, he looks cool.

"I knew he was eager to do a smaller, independent movie. He had already made a few of the bigger Hollywood movies, where he spent most of his time in a trailer, sitting around waiting to work. I knew he wanted to get back to his roots, so to speak."

Banderas, who has said it was like-at-first-sight with Rodriguez, has agreed.

"As soon as I read the script, I was interested in the *mariachi* because the part involved a lot of body work. I decided to think in terms of the choreography—to create the character from his body movement more than from the words he speaks. The whole thing is like a ballet and my character moves like a panther. He is also like a bullfighter.

"Also, action heroes are not supposed to be vulnerable but I wanted to show his vulnerability, his struggle and pain, to create different edges in his character. I wanted to give him a soul struggle. He carries his pain constantly but every time he kills, he doesn't feel good, he doesn't make jokes. He's in a nightmare.

"But at the same time, we never thought we were doing something deep and profound. We were creating a cartoon and the visuals were the most important element. I think the movie is very honest about what it is. It is not a pretentious movie. You are supposed to have fun watching it."

Despite grueling conditions, Banderas had the time of his life shooting *Desperado*, which was made in only seven weeks. They filmed in Ciudad Acuna, Mexico, which is situated right across the Rio Grande from Del Rio, Texas, the same location where *El Mariachi* was filmed. The action in the sequel picks up where the original left off, with the musician with no name stalking the evil drug lord who killed his girlfriend and maimed his hand.

In addition to a short shooting schedule, the elements worked against them as well. While filming one gun battle, Banderas suffered through one-hundred-twenty-degree heat while working fourteen-hour days. The gunpowder would get so thick breathing became next to impossible.

Antonio not only did his own singing, but he also insisted on doing his own stunts—which resulted in a sprained foot that required local medical assistance.

"He was adamant he do his own stunts so he did," Rodriguez has said. "Except for one shot where he's pointing a gun with both arms. The camera is where his head should be so he physically could not do it. So that time he said, 'Okay Robert, I'll let you be the right arm, since you made up the character—but never again!' "

The independent flavor of the film reminded Banderas of the old days with Almodovar, working by the seat of his pants.

"There was that same feeling of breaking the

rules and I did need that "I felt like a kid again making one of my first movies.

"The film itself is very romantic, very violent—but yet highly stylized. It's a wonderful movie, very fast, fresh, new, and funny. It's interesting, good entertainment. It's not pretentious. It's exactly what we intended to do. It's like an old-fashioned western and in fact felt like playing cowboys and Indians. In a way, Robert is following in the footsteps of Sam Peckinpah, Sergio Leone, and all the other directors who have done very stylistic westerns.

"It's a new way to understand western and action movies. It's a re-creation. We're living in a period of time, in a postmodern era that is more about re-creating than creating. We're looking to the past and taking things we can create—and this happens not only in movies, but in fashion, in painting, and in all the arts."

But as Banderas was quickly learning, things are seldom simple in Hollywood, especially in the current political climate of the country. Because he was the star of the film, he was personally called to task for the movie's undeniably high violence quotient.

The body count became something of a joke during filming. In a display of his black sense of humor, Rodriguez kept track of the film's casualties with a chart he kept on the set lined with the following headings: Killed to Date, To Be Killed Today, and Yet to be Killed. The sheer amount of blanks being fired everywhere gave Banderas pause, mostly a reaction to his awareness of Brandon Lee's accidental death after being shot with a prop gun on the set of *The Crow*.

"I didn't count them, but I think I blew away eighty-one guys." Antonio smiled. "But it must be obvious that we are making fun of all the violence. It's a joke. It's so over-the-top that it becomes cartoon opera.

"And you know, I've been killed onscreen more than I've killed people. I love human beings. I couldn't hurt a fly."

But joking aside, Banderas has some strong opinions about all the posturing being done by American politicians on the issue of violence in films. Coming from a country that suffered under a dictatorship that curbed free speech and ideas, Antonio bristles at the mere impression of censorship.

"People here say movies are too violent. But if we have to forbid violence, then that means we would need to forbid *Hamlet* and *Macbeth* and even *Romeo and Juliet*. And what about the works of Homer and Sophocles? I guess those would have to be taken away as well.

"I am not a philosopher or a sociologist but I like to think about these sorts of things. I respect my freedom—and the freedom of others. I think the mores of society are often very hypocritical and pathetic."

Director Rodriguez has said he appreciates Banderas's views, but at the time he was making the movie, he was simply relieved to have somebody of Banderas's stature and abilities carrying his film.

"Working with Antonio was amazing," Rodriguez all but gushed. "When I first met him, he had such energy and passion and I couldn't believe nobody had shot him that way. He can just melt the screen with his presence. I was working with an extremely experienced actor but it was almost like I pulled him off another planet because nobody had seen him in an action film so he was someone new and exciting."

Rodriguez can be forgiven for sounding as if he discovered Banderas—the young director has yet to hit thirty and has the young *auteur's* ego. Although it is true that the movie "action hero" was one of the few cinematic roles Banderas had yet to conquer. Simply because he hadn't tried. And typically, when given the chance he infused the *mariachi* with his own unique stamp.

"The character in the original movie became a killer by accident." Banderas explained. "He's just a nice guy who wants to play guitar and sing songs and make some money. He writes his lyrics and music and is happy. He's a romantic, who suddenly finds himself in the crossfire. They confuse him with someone else and he ends up having to kill people—but he isn't really like that. At the end of the movie, they've killed the woman he loves and shot him in the hand so he can't play guitar anymore.

"The character Robert and I created for *Desperado* is a guy who is only thinking about revenge. He is a man with a pain in his soul. He's solitary and has become another person than who he was before. This time, he's not carrying a guitar in his case, he's carrying a guitar case full of weapons. He wears a black suit with skulls. He's not a normal guy. You know he's not looking for justice, he only thinks about getting even—'They're not going to mess with me anymore. I'm going to kick their asses.'

"He knows he's not on the right track but he has to do it. This feeling is stronger than himself, this feeling he got after they killed his woman. On the other hand, he's very religious. He says a line I like a lot. When he knows that he's going to a place where he probably has to kill somebody or he can be killed, he always crosses himself and says, 'Give me the strength to be what I want and forgive me for what I am.'

"The *mariachi* is a guy who is more in your mind than reality. He has become like a samurai. He's become epic, he has become romantic and he has to be totally this way."

The movie does boast a couple of redemptive moments, such as the scene where, in the middle of a gunfight, the *mariachi* risks his own life to save a little boy from being killed. And the ending is almost hopeful. As the hero drives away with

Salma Hayek in his Jeep, he throws his guitar case full of weapons away onto the road.

But a few moments later, the Jeep backs up and he retrieves his weapons.

"Just in case." He smiles at the camera.

"I think the Latin community has finally got an action hero," Antonio has said.

Definitely not the buzz-cutted, "Yo, I am da law," semiilliterate type personified by Stallone et al, Banderas has turned the action hero image on its side and made it his own. His hero has murderous flair and a definite sense of style. Antonio has traded the meaty brawn of Schwarzenegger for a more refined superiority.

"I probably borrow more from flamenco dancers and bullfighters than from the *Terminator*," Banderas has chuckled. "Robert and I rescued things from Spanish culture to make the character elegant. Even his long hair. Mine is normally curly but we wanted it flat for the movie to make it graceful in slow motion."

In addition to starring a Latin as the hero, *Desperado* also broke some other rules along those lines, mostly with the casting of Mexican film star Salma Hayek as Banderas's love interest.

"They always say the door is closed to ethnics in Hollywood," Rodriguez has said when discussing his film on-line. "I find that the best way in through a closed door is to kick it open. But you have to keep doing it because it slams back at you.

"I know there was resistance to put Salma in the movie by people who had closed minds. They wanted to cast a blonde in the role. But I thought it was important for there to be a Latin heroine in a Latin movie. That's why you have to make your own movies, so that you can show rather than tell. It's more powerful to demonstrate what you can do than to say what you can do."

Antonio had already shown what he could do onscreen. What he proved with *Desperado* was that he *could* carry a movie, *muchas gracias*. The movie was a hit with the fans and most critics recognized its likable appeal. One reviewer summed up the movie's strengths and weaknesses this way:

"The plot has all the sophistication of a dime store novel cover. But here, as with John Woo's ballistic orgies, the gunplay *is* the story. The characters use their bullets like words, as an instant communiqué of rage and will. Rodriguez organizes even the quietest scenes around the playful threat of violence: A tattooed brute pushing the buttons of a pay phone with the point of his knife; a bedroom montage with Banderas gently running his spurs over the delectable curves of his new lover.

"The flourishes are so brazen, they're funny. The movie's greatest visual coup, though, is Banderas himself. The camera loves this velvet stud as much as it did the young Clint Eastwood. With long, straight dark hair that matches his matador-cowboy outfits and a stare as hot as lava, he's an icon of feral, strutting vengeance."

Yeowza!

Salma Hayek, who calls Banderas intense and passionate, did point out that she too went above and beyond the call of duty for the sake of that boot spur scene, one of the film's most memorable images.

"I was sitting in my hotel room, located in the middle of nowhere, and suddenly realized I had this major love scene the next day," Hayek has recalled. "Antonio was going to be intimate with my legs and thighs all day so I decided to arrange to have my legs waxed. So I called down to the desk and they sent over three girls from the local salon.

"They were supposedly the best but it turned out they had never waxed a leg before—only *mustaches*! I was screaming from the pain. It took them over two hours and by the end I just collapsed on the bed. But, my legs looked great in the scene and that's all that mattered."

As Banderas as action hero made audiences swoon, even normally staid reviewers got caught up in the fun. *Newsweek* couldn't ignore his star power.

"This movie's a great showcase for Banderas's soulful, and soulfully funny, swashbuckling. He invests this action role with a flamenco dancer's grace and a brooding sensuality that has inspired comparison to Valentino."

Valentino again. That name was beginning to give him a pain. Antonio could only shake his head.

"In terms of casting, they try to put me in a cage or a box to determine what the hell I am—you know Antonio Banderas, the Latin Lover.

"It's funny, there's always that thing following me around. It's nothing that I am pushing. I've been looking at myself in the mirror for thirty-five years and I've lost objectivity of what I am. My work is in the technique of being a good actor.

"I never thought of myself as a star or a hunk or a heartthrob or any other name you have for it. On one hand, though, I'll probably be seen as that Latin Lover type forever. I don't push that image but after all this time I must accept it. It doesn't worry me. I mean, it is only a question of time before I start getting older. Even if I get greasy and fat and lose my hair, they'll cast me and say, 'Yes, but he *was* a Latin Lover.'

"I have been pretty fortunate to play a wide range of roles, from a tormented artist to a homosexual to a vampire and now to an action hero. Next I may have the opportunity to sing. Everything is good if you are open to learn from it."

And if you have time to reflect on it. But time was a precious commodity for Antonio, who just kept on working.

Following *Desperado* Banderas was committed to three more movies, to be filmed in quick succession. First up was the thriller *Never Talk to Strangers* with Rebecca DeMornay, followed by *Two Much*, a romantic comedy with Melanie Griffith and lastly, *Assassins*, opposite Sylvester Stallone.

For as much of an impact as *Desperado* made, *Never Talk to Strangers* came and went with hardly a whimper, which surprised Banderas. He thought the film was a tight little thriller that would have a nice run. And in it, Banderas got to be the bad guy again.

"It was a thriller with a lot of surprises, like the way Hitchcock used to surprise and manipulate his audiences. I thought the audience would be very intrigued by the plot in the same way. My character is supposed to be a particular way but it turns out he may be very different. He provokes the woman, played by Rebecca DeMornay, into a relationship, which she regrets as soon as she begins to find out what kind of guy he is. Or thinks he is. I just love those kind of mysteries, playing a good guy who's portrayed as a bad guy for the whole film."

As usual, Banderas left a wake of warm feelings in his trail. Rebecca DeMornay, who has worked with some of Hollywood's biggest macho men, like

Tom Cruise in *Risky Business*, thought Banderas was one of a rare breed.

"Antonio takes himself a lot less seriously than a lot of American actors," she noted wryly. "It's not that he's unaware that he's an attractive man—he's not stupid. But he doesn't place any great importance on it."

Interesting comment, considering that the same has been said of DeMornay, an actress who has spent considerable time in interviews downplaying her own celebrated looks.

Within a few weeks of wrapping *Never Talk to Strangers*, Antonio found himself on an airplane heading for Miami where the romantic comedy *Two Much* was to film. In it, Banderas plays a con man who pretends to have a twin brother in order to romance two different women simultaneously. One of the ladies is Daryl Hannah, the other Melanie Griffith.

"I create this other brother just so I'm free to pick up the other girl. It's a funny movie, I think, because he's trapped by his own game. It's too much for him."

Banderas was excited for a couple of reasons. First, the movie was to be directed by fellow Spaniard Fernando Trueba. Second, he would have the chance to work with Griffith, one of his favorite American actresses.

"*Working Girl* was a big hit in Spain. Plus, you always saw pictures of her in the magazines with

Don Johnson, who is very popular in Spain. *Miami Vice* was very big back at home. My only thought going into the movie was that it would be a fun, easy set. I still remembered being introduced to her at the Oscars my first trip to America and was excited to be meeting her again."

Little did he know just how excited. Had Banderas been able to see the future, one wonders if he would have packed his bags and run back to Spain—or if he'd have met his destiny head on. But Antonio was no seer, so he went to work as he always had, never expecting that this otherwise unremarkable role in an unspectacular movie would so thoroughly change his life.

— CHAPTER TEN —

It had started out so simply, just like any other movie set.

"Sometimes you are working with an actress and you get infatuated by the image of the character they are playing. That does happen," Banderas has readily admitted. "Like when I did *The House of the Spirits* and my character falls in love with Winona Ryder's character. I found myself really caring. It took me a while to get over that. You get wrapped up in the image and the story. But it's not that you have to go to bed with her. It's just that you like her and at the end of the day, you both leave and go home to your families or boyfriends or whatever.

"Because everybody knows set romances just can't happen and be real, right?

"Well, with Melanie, I liked her immediately. I

remembered having seen her at the Oscars when I was in town for *Women on the Verge of a Nervous Breakdown*, so when I got on the set, I went over and introduced myself. I was really looking forward to working with her because I respect her talent as an actress.

"At first, we were just speaking politely. We were laughing together and spending time together on the set, making jokes and talking about our real lives in between takes. Then one day I asked her how old she was. Melanie looked at me and told me that was no question to ask a lady.

"I was so embarrassed, I blushed." Antonio closed his eyes at the memory. "Then she smiled and looked at me and said, 'I'm thirty-seven.' And I said, 'That's fine.' And after that, I don't know, something wonderful happened. The more we talked, as the days passed, I realized little by little I was feeling more and more about this person. Real feelings.

"But," he added forcefully, "this wasn't really a set romance because *nothing* happened on the set."

Banderas swears his relationship with Griffith was platonic during the time they were in Miami filming the movie but whether they failed to consummate the relationship because of honorable or logistical reasons is debatable. Both Don Johnson and Ana joined their respective spouses on location, making for one awkward foursome—whether Don and Ana knew it or not.

"I swear, we were honestly trying to respect our marriages and our spouses. And I'll say it again, nothing happened at that time. But we knew something was happening inside," Banderas has said, tapping his chest. "I remember Melanie coming into my trailer and we were laughing about how odd everything was, but nothing, *really nothing*, happened—in terms of sex.

"When Don and Ana left, this thing between us, though, it kept growing. But then too soon, the movie was over. I was so sad when that day came. But the movie was done so we finished and we said good-bye to each other. And that seemed to be the end of it. I was starting a new movie and I had begun to convince myself that what I was feeling was probably an illusion that was going to go away as soon as I started the new movie. Or went back to see my wife.

"But it didn't. Melanie and I started calling each other and talking a lot on the phone. Then we saw each other again and that was it. I knew right then I was really, really in love."

And he had a really, really big problem.

It's in keeping with his character that Antonio jumped in both feet first without stopping to think how deep the water may be. In his mind, he had *no choice* but to follow his heart. Almost immediately, rumors began swirling that Melanie Griffith had a new beau, that Spanish heartthrob Antonio. There were sightings of the couple at the Peninsula

Hotel in Beverly Hills and other places but everybody through their publicists hotly denied that Banderas and Griffith were involved or that Antonio had left his wife. Someone even put out the word that the Antonio-Melanie match-up was a publicity ploy for *Two Much*.

But living a lie and a double life does not come naturally for Antonio. If he was to follow his heart, he would do so openly and honestly—and let the chips fall where they may. This was a man *seriously* in love and he was ready to tell the world.

In Hollywood the months between December and March are known as the Awards Season, when any group even remotely associated with television and film hands out kudos. Awards Season usually culminated in March with the Oscars but each year, a new group announced itself in the "off award season" and tonight it was the Blockbuster Video Awards, which was honoring the video rental audience's favorite stars and movies.

The regular gaggle of West Coast *paparazzi* milled around like restless cattle in their photo pen, an area roped off by red velvet sashes that ran parallel to the red-carpeted walkway upon which the celebrities would make their entrance. Further away, spectators were kept in a more remote spot, safely away from the stars they came to see.

Although the Blockbuster Video Awards was not a major event by anybody's standard, it still had enough juice to command a respectable showing of

A- and B-list stars. The Blockbuster chain is America's largest renter of videos, and studios, well aware of the money generated by the video audience, strongly urged stars of their movies to show support for the new Awards. Besides, a party is a party.

Tonight, however, promised to be more interesting than usual because tonight promised a photo-op coup. The rumor mill had been working overtime all day and by the time the photographers lined up, flashes and lenses at the ready, the word was out: Tonight was the night Melanie Griffith and her new hunk-o-love Antonio Banderas would finally go public with what everyone else had known for weeks. They were Hollywood's hottest new couple.

For Melanie, it was a symbolic out with the old, in with the new. After nearly a year of watching her second-time-around marriage to one-time *Miami Vice* star Don Johnson die a slow, agonizing death, she had finally said good-bye for good to Don and set her sights on a life partner.

But it was trickier for Antonio. Mostly because of a little complication back in Spain—his wife. Banderas, who had become America's favorite new foreign-born son over the matter of a few short years, was suddenly in the unenviable position of wanting to trumpet his new passion with Griffith to the world, while being all-too-aware that in doing so he might very well come across like an all-star, international cad. But what could he do? He was wildly, madly, head over heels in love with his blonde American princess.

"I did not leave my wife for Melanie," he said to all who asked, a phrase that would become his mantra over the following months. "It's not like I met this girl and *boom*. But I did fall in love. And you cannot go against love.

"It's in my nature," Banderas tried to explain better. "I am a Leo so I fall hard and love big. I am passionate and generous—and sometimes I am too passionate and too generous. I fall in love with my whole body, every cell. I don't have shields protecting me. I am very much naked to everything I do in my life. And sometimes that can be strange. Sometimes the thing is just leading me along, and suddenly it's, 'Oh, my God, am I the only one loving this thing?'—whether we're talking about a movie I'm working on or the person I'm in love with.

"But in Melanie's case, I think I put everything on the table before I took a position. I don't think it's for everybody, just to break up a relationship. But this was not an impulse on our parts. It was meditated."

That was part of the problem. Many of Banderas's fans seem somewhat shell-shocked—okay, many are downright horrified—that Antonio, a deep-thinking actor trained in the classics, should fall for one of America's bubble-gum, lightweight actresses.

Say it ain't so, Antonio.

The term bimbo has occasionally been cruelly tossed about. And that's from people claiming to like Melanie. Her detractors are even less kind about her motives. But Banderas has riled at any suggestion their love is anything but pure—and spiritual.

"Some people have said to me, 'Antonio, you were so perfect in the public's eye. You were a faithful husband and a happily married man in a marriage that seemed to be working wonderfully.' But that's all it was—seeming to be.

"Nor did I steal Melanie from Don Johnson. This is a step that Melanie took for her life. She doesn't belong to me, she never belonged to anybody. And if someday she finds someone more interesting than me, or if our relationship is not going good or whatever, then I will have to hand over that, too. I never believed in that belonging thing.

"If I passed up happiness in my life just out of fear that my image might suffer, *that* would be dirty. That would be really, really dishonest. If I have to sacrifice fans, if anyone would say, 'Oh, Antonio, this is not the right move,' I would say, 'Well, fuck you!' "

Banderas composed himself.

"I mean, I wouldn't actually *say* that, but what I would say, and what I feel, is that it's not your life!

It's my life! And my happiness. And I have to decide for myself."

And Antonio decided to damn the career torpedoes and push straight ahead. He would follow his heart and live honestly, refusing to hide his love for Griffith. The thought of sneaking around, dodging press and photographers like illicit lovers was too distasteful . . . and disrespectful of both Melanie and their *amor*.

"We decided to go public on that particular night because if you don't come clean, the press starts to have fantasies that are wilder than the truth," Banderas has said. "They had already begun inventing things about Melanie and me, for example, saying our togetherness was simply a publicity stunt for our movie, *Two Much*. I also heard that Melanie was already pregnant, that we were going to have to get married, all sorts of lies."

So on that summer evening, Banderas and Griffith raised the temperature by stepping out together, heads held high. Well, at least when their heads came up for air. The two lovebirds spent so much time kissing, veteran shutterbugs began laying bets whether Antonio or Melanie would get a cramp in their necks—or lips—first.

"It came across as an in-your-face, rubbing our noses in it display," comments one journalist who witnessed the love-fest up close and personal. "I'm not saying they don't feel passionately for one another, but it was interesting to notice that they weren't nearly as stuck together later on at the after-party, which was held across the street at the Palace. There, they more or less just held hands most of the evening."

But even togetherness has its practical drawbacks.

"It was pretty amusing watching them try to eat while still holding hands."

Interestingly, Banderas's decision to come clean about what most Hollywood pundits at the time were calling his extramarital affair, somehow just further cemented his reputation as America's very own Latin Lover of the 90s. By refusing to concede that he and Melanie had done anything wrong, he gave their relationship a measure of dignity it otherwise would not have had. Although that dignity would be sorely tested in the months to come.

As Banderas sat through the Blockbuster Awards, he often had a faraway look in his eyes—an "Alice in Wonderland glaze." How on earth had one of Spain's most respected actors ended up the new darling of the tabloid press in America? Or had his whole life just been a dress rehearsal for this tragicomic latest act currently being played out? He didn't know. All he was sure of was that it used to be a lot less complicated than this.

The fallout from their first public date was predictable. The tabloids had a field day. Melanie and Antonio's every meeting of the lips was faithfully reproduced in living color. Now that their romance was out in the open, it seemed as if everybody wanted in on it. And not only the press. Banderas has recalled being chased down the Los Angeles freeway by video camera-toting tourists, determined to get him and Melanie on tape.

"I have no doubts it would have ended up on one of the tabloid television shows," Banderas sighed when recalling the incident. "All the attention was not good. It forced me to do crazy things."

Like hit the pedal to the metal in Griffith's Porsche in order to literally outrun their pursuers. Even for someone who has spent his entire adult life in the public eye like Banderas has, the intense interest in his love life threw Banderas for an astounded loop.

Not only did his picture grace the covers of the newspaper tabloids, from the *National Enquirer* to the *New York Post*, but the burgeoning field of broadcast tab-TV shows made Antonio and Melanie their favorite sound-bite couple. The constant stream of coverage became claustrophobic.

"We were simply trying to do things in the best way possible, with integrity, dignity, and honesty," Antonio has said, sounding at the time as if he still needed convincing. "You know, we thought something would happen when we went public, that there would be interest—but not as big as it became. In terms of making noise, we figured it would be maybe a five—and it turned out to be one hundred. I thought it was a storm that would pass quickly, once everyone got bored."

Think again, *hombre*. Public interest refused to go quietly into that great celebrity good night.

His personal tumult made Banderas, at least for a while, a man without a home. Because he had always considered himself first and foremost Spanish, he never bothered to buy a house in Los Angeles, even though his time in California increased every year since 1991. For a while, because of previous film commitments, Banderas and Griffith would make respective film locations their homes away from home together.

Antonio was experiencing both heaven and hell—he was with the woman he loved but his future with Melanie was on hold until he resolved the past with Ana. He had never dreaded anything more in his life.

— CHAPTER ELEVEN —

In the winter of 1995, Griffith wasn't that settled, either. Despite having two children she was also between permanent homes. She had just extracted herself at long last from her marriage to Don Johnson and in an attempt to cut ties for good, had uprooted the kids. The split had been painfully drawn out. A year earlier, Melanie had tried filing for divorce only to have Johnson in essence refuse to accept it. He was so adamant they not break up, she agreed to reconcile, but in the end, nothing was resolved and Griffith finally bolted, giving up their California digs in the process.

But now that she had attached her wagon to Banderas, she was feeling homey again, apparently much to the delight of her children. Alexander, ten, from her marriage to actor Steve Bauer, and her son with Johnson, Dakota, now six, by all accounts were charmed by Banderas.

"The kids took the last breakup between Don and Melanie really hard," a longtime family friend has said. "They'd broken up so many times it was a shock for the boys to realize this time it was for keeps. I actually think Antonio came to the rescue in a way. He's very emotional and very open, so the kids related to him. He's like a kid in many ways himself. And he really is so very sweet. He naturally feels concern and care for the boys if for no other reason than they are Melanie's babies. He's so blown away by her he loves them by osmosis.

"But it's never easy at first when a new person comes into a family setting so Antonio put a lot of effort into winning the kids over. He made it clear that he didn't want to take their mom away—he wanted to share her. He didn't want to take their place in her heart, he wanted a place made for him, too. He made himself as nonthreatening as possible, because Antonio is in this for the long haul."

"It definitely was hard in the beginning," Antonio has agreed when asked. "We had to have a lot of conversations, especially with Alexander. He's the oldest so he's the one who is most aware of what is going on. So I really talked to him. I told him, 'We have to put all the bad feelings you have inside on the table. You have to let them out. I want you to tell me exactly what you are feeling, what you are thinking. It is important to me.

" 'And you can say anything—I'm not going to get upset or mad.' I wanted him to know I would try to understand what he was feeling. I remember being a kid like it was yesterday and I remember feeling such pain inside and crying because nobody understood how I felt. Nobody talked to me about it. I did not want that for him, so we talked and let it all out in the open."

Children are seldom fooled by pretense so it's a testament to Banderas's sincerity that he was able to reach the youngster. And that the youngster reached back.

"We worked it out and now it's wonderful. It's gorgeous when I'm sitting down and all of a sudden he jumps on me and then rests his head on my shoulder. It just makes my heart fill. He looks up to me, he *counts* on me now. He calls me and says, 'Antonio, I need you.' I tell you, it makes me cry and smile at the same time inside. I just *love* that."

The same little boy who refused to relinquish his boots in bed displayed that same stubborn streak when it came to bowing to criticism of his love affair with Griffith. Rather than plead *mea culpa* to the decision to leave his wife, Banderas maintained the rightness of following his heart.

"There is not a connection between the breaking up of my marriage with Ana and my relationship with Melanie. People are saying I was unfaithful, that I left my wife for a celebrity and things like that, which are not true."

But Banderas is not a fool and he knows that's exactly what it looked like to an outsider looking in. Hell, it's no doubt what it looked like to Ana. And even some of Antonio's friends have voiced cautious curiosity about his relationship with Griffith.

"I would have never put Antonio with Melanie," his *Desperado* costar Salma Hayek offered. "He seems to be very happy but I think one thing Antonio particularly likes about Melanie is that she's so representative of Hollywood and America.

"He just loves Hollywood so much—you should hear him talk about the people he would meet. He gets all excited and almost starstruck. It just seems that Melanie fits right into that whole scene, you know?"

Banderas is aware that some people think attaching himself to Griffith was an inspired career move.

"I knew there would be people who would accuse me of being sucked in by Hollywood, of going with Melanie because I think it will make me a bigger Hollywood star or more accepted here," Banderas has admitted. "But they are wrong. If that's what I was interested in, I could have done that with Madonna. But the difference is I fell in love with Melanie. I was not in love with Madonna."

His inability to understand what makes their relationship so fascinating to the general public offers an interesting insight into Banderas. While most people would do exactly what he did and leave a lifeless, childless marriage given the opportunity, few would feel so outwardly righteous about it. It was *unseemly* to take such a noble posture. Here he was, living a charmed life and the woman he'd been with before he was anybody was being left in the dust. It seemed so . . . typical. Like the middle-aged businessman dumping his matronly wife for the sexy bimbo secretary.

"Believe me, it has not been easy," Antonio has said. "I understand I'm a public person but I've always been very respectful of others and I'd like to be treated in the same way.

"The best thing to do is to not give in by becoming a media circus player. Especially because Melanie has two children who we feel the desire to protect. But on the other hand if you try to fight the mass media system, it can destroy you. The best thing you can do is put the weapon down. We don't have anything to hide. We've said, 'Hey, here we are. Yes, we're in love.'

"But it's awful to be justifying yourself in the public eye. I can't believe the fact that we fell in love is still considered news. But the truth is not what worries me, it's the untruths. But I can't, and won't, let the lies being printed in the newspapers make me angry. I prefer to take it with a sense of humor.

"Here I am, just trying to enjoy my life and this

wonderful thing that's happened to me. But instead of wishing us well, I am aware there are people actually making bets on how long Melanie and I will be together."

Antonio angrily put out his cigarette with a frustrated twist of his hand.

"Okay, I'll cover those bets. I'll take that chance even though I know I might lose. Nothing is a sure thing. And if this relationship ends some day, I'll be alone. But I'll know that I tried to keep the flame alive and make the other person happy. That's all I can do. And for that, people feel free to throw hammers at our faces?

"And it's not just the Americans. My own press, in Spain, they make comments like 'Melanie and Antonio, Stop It!' For me fine, I wish it would stop right now. But there is nothing, *nothing* possibly you can do. I can accept any kind of review, any kind of criticism because you learn from that. But these kinds of articles that say you are a pimp, it's something I don't understand."

It's because nobody is supposed to be that talented, that good-looking and that passionately I-try-but-it's-impossible-for-me-to-take-my-hands-off-of-you in love. But even from the beginning, it was clear Antonio was going to be unique among his peers.

What Antonio wanted more than anything was for people—his fans, his friends, his family—to be happy for him. If they thought he was a jerk, so be it, but something about being made to appear foolish in print, to be patronized by puff-piece magazines, really got under his skin.

"One day we went with Melanie's kids to the airport because they were going back to Los Angeles," Banderas has said when interviewed, lighting one of his ever-present cigarettes. "And we pick up an issue of *People* magazine to flip through. Suddenly, I see two pages filled with different pictures of me and Melanie kissing each other from different places. They ran a headline in big, big words: OH, STOP IT ALREADY!

"If this is advice, of course I'm not going to take it from *People* magazine." He rolled his eyes. "Listen, I'm going to kiss my girlfriend as much as I want in the places I want because, fortunately, in America it's not forbidden yet.

"But I do have some advice for them. If you are so bored with it then why don't you stop and not use those pictures?"

Maybe Europeans don't mind when celebrities act like teenagers with runaway hormones in public. But the American Puritan streak tends to react badly to people who revel in their passion in mixed company. Antonio was learning the lesson that Americans really did prefer you keep it behind closed doors—even if they liked to peek in on occasion.

The summer of 1995 brought record heat across

the country, a perfect environment for America's most-talked about star. It was gearing up to be an important summer movie season for Banderas, with some major releases due out, including *Assassins* with Sylvester Stallone and *Desperado.*

It was gut-check time. How would America respond to Banderas as a hit man? Could he carry *Desperado* on his marquee value alone? Would there be fan backlash to his affair with Griffith? Raising a few eyebrows was the fact that as of June, neither Antonio nor Ana had actually filed for divorce. A situation not lost on Melanie's friends.

"Everyone was telling Melanie, she better watch out, that Antonio might be setting her up for a fall," says a friend of the actress. "Melanie just laughed and assured everybody Antonio wasn't planning on running back to his wife any time soon. Antonio was just keeping the ball in Ana's court. He wanted to at least give her the opportunity to be the one who filed the papers. It was a kind of face-saving gesture, which Ana no doubt saw as way too little, way too late."

Melanie and Antonio were at the stage of their togetherness when they were at least coming up for air now and then. It was time to start integrating each other into the broader spectrum of their lives. It was easier for Melanie on this front than for Antonio—her marriage was over and nobody was accusing Banderas of being a home-wrecker. So Melanie happily set about showing Antonio off to

ANTONIO BANDERAS

her friends out at dinner and functions.

"He's just the nicest guy," says one pal. "In fact, he's almost too good to be true. How come they don't make them that way here in America?"

Melanie was not shy about expressing her adoration for Antonio in bubbly sound bites.

"He's so alive, so *wild*," she gurgled. "I love his voice, I love the way he looks at the world. And I really admire him as an actor. He doesn't go by anybody's rules. You never know what's going to come out of his mouth. Never, ever. And it's the same in real life, too. You know what Antonio is like? He's like an explosion."

Among the most important people Antonio met was Melanie's mom, actress Tippi Hedren. Wanting everything to be perfect, Melanie had carefully planned for her and Antonio to spend an entire weekend at her mom's ranch in Sylmar, a community located about an hour north of Los Angeles. She wanted Antonio and her mom to get to know each other.

But the visit to mama's ranch didn't go exactly as planned. In fact, Antonio saw his life flash before his eyes when he came face to face with an overly playful adult male lion. Griffith had told Banderas about her mother's love of animals but it never really sank in when she said her mom owned some big cats.

"Antonio's thinking, chubby house cats," laughs a friend.

Hedren, best known for her work in Alfred Hitchcock's *The Birds* and *Marnie*, has turned her ranch, called Shambala, into a sanctuary for a menagerie of over sixty lions, tigers, and panthers which she has adopted. She also has a few elephants. Most of the animals are either retired from the movies or former circus performers, some of which Tippi rescued from squalid conditions.

It was a beautiful, clear day, the kind that makes it easy to see why settlers flocked to the California coast hundreds of years ago. Melanie and Antonio drove up to the ranch on a Friday, with plans to stay the entire weekend.

"It was supposed to be a wonderfully romantic getaway, even if they were going to Melanie's mom's house," says a friend. "They were going to go horseback riding, have picnics, watch the sun set, and take walks hand in hand. They really do approach things like teenagers, but that's how they are.

"Anyway, Melanie made a big show of introducing Tippi to Antonio and of course, he turned on the charm. He told Tippi now he understood where Melanie got her beauty from and thanked her for bringing Melanie into the world. After they chatted for a while inside, Tippi asked Antonio if he'd like to see her animals. Naturally, he said yes."

Hedren has worked with animals for years, ever since retiring from films so Griffith grew up around the felines and was very comfortable in their presence. Antonio, on the other hand, had only ever appreciated big beasts from afar, in circuses and zoos so he was wide-eyed as they neared the cats.

"Tippi loves her animals so of course she wanted Antonio to meet one up close and personal," says the friend. "She picked her favorite lion. Although Tippi usually has some handlers working for her, on this particular occasion she decided to bring the lion out herself.

"But suddenly, the big cat lunged away from Tippi and she lost her grip on the rope. The lion loped directly toward Antonio, probably because the animal had never seen Antonio before so he was a new person to sniff and get to know."

But all Banderas saw was a huge fang-bearing, muscle-bound, sharp-toothed lion charging right for him.

"It happened so fast, Antonio only had time to raise his arms in front of his face. He was so stunned, he didn't even make a noise when the lion jumped up and knocked him to the ground. He just curled into a little ball and started praying in Spanish. But that was it. The lion wasn't trying to hurt Antonio, it turns out it was just playing. The same way a dog will jump up to play when it meets someone new. Basically, it was just an overgrown kitty. Plus, it was declawed so Antonio didn't so much as get a scratch on him."

Hedren admitted in an interview once that the

lion was just exhibiting a pussy-cat sense of humor.

"One lion does think it's hilarious to tackle us. He's very funny about it."

Banderas, however, was not amused.

"Even though he tried to maintain his own sense of humor about the incident, Antonio was more than a little freaked out," says the friend. "So much so that it kind of put a damper on the weekend. Part of it, I'm sure was that Antonio was embarrassed that he had reacted as if he was about to be lunch. Here he was trying to make a good impression, and ends up on the ground in a fetal position.

"So Melanie and Antonio cut the weekend short and wound up driving back to Los Angeles that night. I guess he decided he'd take the Hollywood jungle any day."

Despite the mishap, for Tippi's money, Antonio is a wonderful guy.

"I'm thrilled he's made my daughter as happy as he has," she has said with a mom's pragmatism. "I wish them all the best."

Banderas was looking forward to a break from his real life. After figuratively and literally enduring the heat in L.A., Seattle seemed like a wonderful change of pace. Antonio was anxious to delve into his next role, that of an up and coming assassin bent on wiping out the old master, played by Sylvester Stallone. Antonio was also looking forward to a little peace and quiet after being unable to open a magazine for the past half year and not see his face or personal life splashed across the pages.

Seattle and the beauty of the Pacific Northwest brought Banderas much needed peace of mind.

"It looks like the Mediterranean a little bit," he said with an undertone of nostalgia. After being battered and bruised by the international press, Banderas could be forgiven for thinking back to the deserted beaches of his youth.

If nothing else, Antonio seemed to be learning. While still making no secret of their relationship, he and Melanie had started taking a lower-key approach to things, acting less like lusty teenagers and more like adults in love. And to a degree, it seemed to be working. The American press wasn't quite as ever-present as it had been, although Antonio and Melanie were hardly anonymous anytime they went out.

But restraint seemed to be Banderas's new weapon of choice. During an interview with a Seattle journalist, Antonio politely deflected questions of a personal nature.

"I'm so happy in my life, but there are other people involved and I would like to respect them. So Melanie and I have decided it's just too recent, too raw to discuss right now. I am just trying to live as much as possible in the best way I can. In a sense, I think I should enjoy the bad moments, too.

"We have nothing to hide, mind you. I would

love to talk to you about it next time we meet. Can you respect that?''

Just how raw the emotions were for those being left behind was brought painfully home to Antonio during his stay in Seattle. One weekend morning, while Melanie and Antonio were sleeping, a furious pounding on the door startled them out of sleep. The frantic knocking set off an alarm in Antonio's head and he told Melanie to stay put.

''Instinctively, Antonio had a bad feeling about what was behind the door,'' says a friend. ''He cautiously approached the door, wishing the pounding would stop. He called out and asked who it was and his heart sank when he heard his wife's voice call out his name.

''Melanie cringed in the other room. She later told her friends she just wanted to pull the covers up over her head and disappear for a while. This was not going to be pleasant.''

Banderas opened the door and faced Ana, who stood there all raging indignation and hurt. They spoke to each other in Spanish with the awkwardness that can only come when confronted with broken love and dashed hopes.

''Antonio asked what she was doing in Seattle and Ana said she had no choice. Since she couldn't get him to talk to her any other way, she would come to him. She begged him not to throw away all their years together, their history. She reminded him that they were of the same country, the same people, the same blood—bonds that he couldn't have with someone like Melanie. Basically, Ana had traveled half way around the world to ask Antonio to come back to her.

"Antonio kept trying to tell Ana this wasn't the place to talk and tried to make arrangements to see her later, but Ana would not be denied. She told Antonio she forgave him and if he would only come back home, she would never bring it up. They could start over.

"It was almost more than Antonio could bear, seeing Ana groveling like this. He still cared about her so much, but seeing her made him realize that he wasn't in love with her anymore. Still, he didn't want her to be hurt. It was just horrible.

"He told her he couldn't come back home—that their marriage was over. He was in love with Melanie. But he also told Ana that Melanie wasn't the reason he was leaving, that in his heart he had seen them drifting apart for a while, he had just never admitted it to himself. But once he met Melanie, it was time to be honest.

"Antonio was still young, he wanted to be in love again. He didn't want to be in a passionless marriage. But how do you say that to the woman you shared your bed with for nine years. All Antonio could do was apologize and tell her how sorry he was that he had hurt her."

Ana finally left, her trip all for naught. Banderas

stood at the window, looking out at the misty morning. Who would have thought his greatest happiness would be tempered by such melancholy?

— CHAPTER TWELVE —

Despite being rebuked during her impromptu visit to Seattle, Ana wasn't willing to give up. She decided to fight Antonio on his home turf, as it were. She let it be known to papers in Spain that in spite of everything, she *still* didn't want to get a divorce. And she was holding out for one, last desperate shot of holding her marriage together—family intervention.

Her timing was impeccable because Antonio had to return home. It was time he introduced Melanie to his family and it was time to talk to them and explain his feelings. He couldn't avoid it any longer. Antonio's family had been mortified by the way his love life had been splattered in the papers. Not that his family could change anything, but he would prefer to have their blessing rather than not.

The trip to Spain was planned for August and it

was hard to know who was more nervous, Melanie or Antonio. Griffith felt as if she were going into her own lion's den while Antonio felt like the Prodigal Son. But at the same time he was also excited about going back home. He was desperate to show Melanie all the places he had described to her—his hometown, the gorgeous beaches, the wonderful parks—everything he loved about his country.

They both knew it would be awkward at times, but their attitude was, might as well get it over with now so they could get on with their lives. Compared to what they'd already endured in the American press, how bad could it be?

Worse than Antonio could have ever imagined.

The Spanish press made the Americans look like polite schoolboys. Literally every move Antonio made was duly photographed, taped, filmed, and recorded. Griffith was bluntly called a home-wrecker and a whore in print. Ana was hoisted on a pedestal by the press as the long-suffering wife who was holding her head high. Banderas, interestingly, was simply portrayed as confused. Lust-crazed. Deluded by the brassy American blonde. Blinded by his hormones. In other words, it was hard for his countrymen to really hold a grudge against their native son. So instead, Griffith took the brunt of the attack.

Banderas was amazed at the zeal of the press.

"I really think I'm the same guy now that I was before I started working in America. But this time when I come home, I am followed by thirty-five to forty journalists. When Melanie and I went sailing there were six or seven boats with *paparazzi* circling our boat. It got to the point of the ridiculous.

"I did everything to reach them as human beings, even buying them drinks on one of the hottest days. Finally, I reasoned with them. I talked to them man to man. I made a deal. We agreed that they could follow us around five days a week and we would cooperate and pose, but that for two days a week, they leave us alone."

Interestingly enough, it worked.

"I've learned a lot from Antonio and how he handles the press," Melanie has admitted. "He's always so calm that he gets them to be more like people."

But it didn't keep the press from writing about him—and Melanie. Most hurtful to him was the viciousness of the articles that detailed her history of alcohol and substance abuse. A history she's acknowledged publicly.

"I'm not silly. I'm not an idiot," Banderas shot back heatedly. "I love her with everything she brings to it. She has nothing to hide. I'm proud of what she has gone through and overcome. I love this woman and I want to make her happy—that is my only purpose.

"Maybe in terms of my career, our careers, this is a bad move. But what am I supposed to do, not love her because it might be the best thing for my career? That's absurd."

Banderas was also wounded by those who implied the only reason he had dumped his wife for an American movie star was to further his own ambition.

"Some people do think he's changed since he's become a star in Hollywood," Enrique Arias Vega, a Madrid newspaper editor, has said. "They think his character and his attitude, which used to be very approachable and friendly, has changed. Since he's gone to Hollywood, he's different. It's like a drunkenness. He kept drinking in stardom and couldn't get enough."

Banderas felt the need to respond to such criticism.

"Because my career didn't just happen overnight, I've had time to see what's going on around me. I never had a big, great success that I could suddenly be defined by. My progression has been gradual, bit by bit.

"Now that I have had some success, maybe I do play a little with that star thing. I play games. If someone invites me to a party, I might joke around and ask if they are going to send a limousine to pick me up. 'When I am in America, that's what I do so I'm not going to go anywhere without a limo.' It's in fun—but they get scared a little bit, wondering if I'm being serious. But then they realize it's me and say, 'Fuck you. What time will you be here? Oh, and bring some beer.'

"My friends, the real people, they are going to treat me the same. And they are going to treat Melanie like part of my family. That's it. If they start treating me differently, I'll just go, 'Stop it!. I am the same guy who was playing soccer with you in the streets when we were kids.' "

Banderas and Griffith weren't the only ones with press headaches. Antonio's parents were also being hounded by photographers and writers. Watching his father trailed by a line of press, Antonio finally had to laugh.

"This is just too much. Oh, my poor pop. I'm sorry. But you have to laugh. I know the rules of the game I am playing and I have to deal with it. And I choose to deal with it by being able to laugh."

While in Spain, Banderas and Griffith stayed at his house located on the outskirts of Madrid. The property is beautifully lush and the house lavish by any standard, having cost the equivalent in dollars of three hundred thousand. They went to eat at local restaurants, and townsfolk reported their every move to the horde of journalists tailing them.

"Melanie is very beautiful," said one restaurant patron. "She and Antonio ate ham, eggs, and potatoes. And they held hands while eating, too."

Others thought Griffith was not a big eater.

"She didn't seem to like much of the food," said

one server. "But she did try a bowl of the *gazpacho*."

Which just happens to be one of Antonio's favorite foods.

When asked by journalists if his real reason for returning to Spain was to formally introduce Melanie to his parents, Antonio shrugged.

"You know, I haven't seen my parents for a year and a half, but I didn't come to officially introduce everyone."

Banderas had good reason to be vague. The first meeting between his family and Melanie was your basic disaster. Once again, as he had done consistently from the beginning of their affair, Antonio underestimated what the impact of their togetherness would be on others, including his own family. Banderas seems to have forgotten that while he was traveling the world being a star, Ana was back home, with his family, playing the role of the loyally waiting wife. She actually had much more interaction with his family than he did anymore. Much of that was his fault—he had become a citizen of the world and spent very little time in Spain. Now that he was back, he began to wish he hadn't returned.

The low point of their micro-managed vacation was the day Banderas brought Melanie to his parents' home. Griffith knew coming into the trip that there would be plenty of uncomfortable moments. She'd been through breakups and knew the way things worked. Still, not only was she meeting her boyfriend's family for the first time, she was being called a *puta* in the press and was in a country whose language she really didn't speak. Talk about home field disadvantage. Showing her pluck, Griffith went in with a smile. But even an actress has a breaking point and Melanie hit hers.

"If nothing else, Antonio expected his family to be cordial," says a friend. "He wasn't expecting immediate miracles. So he was shocked—and furious—when his family treated Melanie like she was the unclean. They barely said hello to her. Mostly, they just ignored her as if she didn't exist. They made it clear to her that in their minds, she was not part of the family. What made it most hurtful for Melanie is that she'd really been looking forward to meeting Antonio's family and had been hoping they'd at least give her a chance.

"Melanie kept close to Antonio and tried to ignore the slights but finally it got so uncomfortable that Melanie pulled Antonio aside and quietly begged for them to go. Antonio immediately agreed. He was ashamed his family would act so rudely to someone he loved so much. He abruptly made their good-byes and they left.

"As soon as they got outside, Melanie broke down into tears. She cried and cried and there was nothing Antonio could do but hold her and tell her he loved her."

Ironically, the cool family reaction probably had

the opposite effect than the desired one—it made Antonio that much more determined to be with Melanie. Nobody, not even his family would emotionally blackmail him into giving up the woman he loved.

"Antonio's family obviously didn't get that this wasn't a fling," says the friend. "They were looking at it with the typical Latin attitude, if you want to have an affair, fine. But don't flaunt it. Have a mistress, but don't bring her home. They were missing the obvious point that this wasn't a mistress. That this was Antonio's number-one woman. It was just hard for everyone to move on because Ana was still there making it equally clear that she wanted Antonio back."

Banderas firmly told his family that it was his life and he had to do what felt right to him. In other words, he'd appreciate it if they would butt out. He didn't want to have to choose between his family and Melanie—because it would really be a choice between his family and himself and his family would lose.

There was one last thing Banderas wanted to do before leaving Spain—it was time to meet the press head on. If his countrymen had questions, he would answer them. It couldn't be any worse of an experience than confronting his family.

Antonio agreed to be interviewed by a camera crew on his way to dinner on one of his last nights home. The first question hurled at him was whether Hollywood had changed him or was he really the same guy everyone remembered in Málaga.

"I am the same, think so. The people who are saying 'You've changed, 'you've changed, 'you've changed' don't realize that it's not me who's changed, but the things around me have changed. I feel like the same person. I laugh at the same jokes that I did twenty years ago.

"I am living a very fast life in a way. But maybe it's just the lives of the people around me have changed more than I have.

"I have read some articles that have been extremely hard on me and I just don't understand. Of course, there have been people who have talked to me to find out how I breathe. I respect those people but life is very complex. Some people are going to like some things I do, and others are not. But I feel as if I need a break from the press— they've been just way too hard on me."

When asked if he was envied by his peers in Spain, Banderas responded with passion.

"Not at all! In fact, just the other day I read an article written about me where he only expressed gratitude to them. I've always spoken highly of people from my homeland. They are my people. I know full well that there are many actors here who could do the same thing I did. They just chose not to go that way. Some people don't want to work where I have, in the projects I have chosen to do in Hollywood.

"But that's them. For me, Hollywood has been good."

The discussion then moved back to Melanie. The reporter switched gears, asking if Melanie knew any Spanish.

"Yes, she knows a few things, like 'I love you.' And she does love me, what can I say? And there are so many things I love about her. But trying to describe love is like trying to describe life. You know that there is something inside you that is stronger than yourself and it's something you just can't stop.

"Love is such an abstract thing, it's hard to make a concrete list of it's this, this, and this that I love."

The interviewer asked what plans Antonio and Melanie have while they are between movies.

"We'd like to travel a bit and while I'm here, I'd like to meet up with Almodovar and a few other people I've worked with. I'm especially looking forward to introducing Melanie to some of the actors I've worked with and who I shared some very important moments of my life with.

"I'd also like to have the time to visit some museums and just have as quiet of a vacation as possible. I have no interest in going to the hot spots on the coast to mingle with other celebrities. I want to go back and reexperience my country with Melanie.

"You know, there is something curious that happens when you leave your land. It's like when you're looking at a painting. You have to have a certain distance to appreciate it. It's the same with other cultures and other people—you start missing where you really belong.

"Maybe one day Melanie and I will make our home in Spain, I don't know. I don't know what the future holds."

Then came the question all Spain was waiting for—was it hard to leave other relationships. In other words, how does it feel to have dumped your wife?

Antonio knew it was coming and didn't bat an eye.

"Yes, leaving a relationship is difficult, but I never felt any pressure," Banderas said evenly. "There's no real direct correlation that people believe that there is, between me leaving my marriage and going to Melanie Griffith.

"No, I haven't spoken with Ana," he said to the next question. "We're in the process of separating and the easiest way to do that is to keep our distance."

Now the lines had been drawn. The reporter lightly asked Antonio his response to an alleged quote by Don Johnson that Banderas was nothing but a trophy for Melanie. You know, "boy toy." Banderas shrugged.

"It could very well be that I am a trophy for her. But for me, Melanie is a prize."

Griffith at this point piped up that she'd never heard Don say anything like that and would be surprised if he really did. And it's true that for all their very public troubles, Johnson and Griffith have rarely said anything derogatory about the other. They've tried to stay adults for the sake of the kids and have been notably successful.

In an interesting change from their early days out, Banderas objected when the reporter asked the couple to kiss for the camera.

"No, this is not what we want to do."

For those who think American reporters are pushy, they should take a close look at the Spanish fourth estate. Several of the reporters present asked Banderas where he was going. They were worried they would get lost if he made them chase after him blindly. Banderas couldn't believe they're still going to follow him.

"I've really told you everything," he said, exasperated. "We've taken time with you and said so much to you. All I can say is this—we are living one day at a time. What we have is what you see, which is very clear."

Not everything was so traumatic. There were some bright spots, among them his reunion with Pedro Almodovar. The director was immediately taken with Griffith and announced that she was his ideal as an actress.

"She's beautiful," Pedro lavishly told Spanish reporters. "She's the kind of actress I dream about.

And I'm not just saying that to be flattering. She really does have a wonderful quality on film that I admire. In fact, I'm thinking of writing a film for her. She'd be a sensation."

Even if he was being effusive for the sake of his old friend, Griffith was grateful for the positive attention. She and Antonio spent a lot of time with Almodovar during their time in Spain, and Banderas was pleased to see that any old tension between him and the director was gone.

If only others had been so welcoming.

Banderas left Spain a little sad but even more committed to the woman who slept on his shoulder as they flew home.

After the emotionally taxing trip to Spain, it was a relief to come back to the friendlier confines of America. For better or worse, this is where Banderas's life was right now, and apparently his future as well. His relationship with his homeland had become complicated in recent years and Antonio realized that it would not be getting simpler anytime soon. It seemed his destiny called for him to plant roots in America and he decided to heed the call.

Banderas felt his countrymen had behaved badly and it hurt him. And angered him. He was even peeved at Ana. She had not helped, playing the martyr. His wife made it seem as if they had had this perfect marriage until Melanie came along and, like a spider, poisoned everything. Well, that wasn't how it was and Antonio felt the time was finally right for setting that particular record straight.

Banderas knew that his very public personal problems were probably making the studios nervous. A lot was riding on *Desperado* because it was the first film he was "opening." In other words, he was the star and it was his chance to see if his name alone could bring people to the theater. There had been worried whispers wondering if fans may be turned off by his recent notoriety.

But Antonio knew there was nothing he could do about it now. Rather than beat himself up over it, he took a typically European let-the-chips-fall-where-they-may attitude.

"If people think I'm a bad guy because I did what I did, that's fine. What am I going to do? Go house by house explaining to people the reasons why I left my wife? Everybody has problems in their houses. That is the way life is."

All he wanted to do was get on with his, wherever it was headed.

— CHAPTER THIRTEEN —

Neither Banderas nor the studio heads needed to have worried. *Desperado* opened well and proved than Banderas indeed had arrived. He could not only carry a film, but was still as popular as ever among film fans. Considering that *Desperado* was made on a relative shoestring budget, it turned nice profits for the studio and any concerns about the status of Antonio's career were quelled.

Ironically, it was *Assassins* that failed to live up to expectations. The film was a stereotypical Sylvester Stallone vehicle, only made interesting by Banderas, who played an up-and-coming hired assassin who wants to make a name for himself by offing the current master, played by a world-weary Sly.

"Now this character is quite twisted," Antonio laughed. "In fact, he's quite out of his mind! He is very different from me, let's hope. The movie shows not only the exterior violence but this man's inner violence, too. What's going on in his head.

"In terms of other films I've done, I'd say he is the complete opposite of the character in *Desperado*. Because the guy in *Assassins* is a portrait of a real killer who doesn't value human life at all. All he wants to do is play this macabre game with Stallone's character. It was like a deadly chess game."

But it was almost a role that didn't happen. Either because of weariness or because his life had just been turned upside down after falling in love with Griffith, Banderas had done a rare thing—he originally turned the film down. Or at least tried to.

"I wanted a break so when Richard Donner called and asked me about *Assassins*, I said thank you, but no. Except, he wouldn't take no for an answer," Antonio recalled.

"He told me that we'd have fun and that it would be an easy shoot so finally I gave in and said yes."

While Banderas did enjoy himself, it wasn't all a picnic.

"I got hit a lot," Banderas said. "And one time, I got a black eye. The stunt guy was supposed to fall on a bed that I was hiding under. When he hit the bed, it broke and I got hit in the face with the gun I was holding. But, I think Sly was proud of me."

As he does on his *Lethal Weapon* movies, Donner keeps the set easy and relaxed. He recognizes that they're just grown men playing games and treats the work accordingly. In this case, more than just the shoot-em-up script brought his *Lethal Weapon* days to mind.

"The first time I met Antonio, I came away with the same feeling as when I met Mel Gibson," the director has said. "They are so much alike that it's incredible. They have that same insanity, the same sensitivity, and the same off-the-wallness. There's this energy, this excitement about everything they say and do.

"This kid is going to be around a long time."

Donner also took Banderas's hotter-than-thou romance with Griffith, who was on the set, in stride.

"Yeah, I just kept a bucket of ice water around and poured in on Antonio when it was time for him to work."

Julianne Moore, the token female in *Assassins*, has said that she counts herself as a Banderas fan.

"Antonio really jumps out at you in this movie. His appeal is just insidious. The best movie stars are those people that you can almost feel the heat coming off of—and Antonio has that."

Banderas has admitted that all the death and mayhem of back-to-back bloody movies did eventually have an effect on him. He became obsessed with thoughts of death in general and his own demise in particular.

"I think we all have to prepare for and accept our own deaths," he mused. "But preparing for death, I think, makes us appreciate life all that much more. Even with all its problems and controversies and pain and struggles I love life."

As with many things in life, Banderas realized that time was the best solution, the best cure. He and Griffith spent much of late 1995 in North Carolina, where she was filming the remake of *Lolita*, taking over the Shelley Winters role of the wronged housewife.

It had been a wild year and from the perspective of an Atlantic Ocean beach, Antonio felt he had traveled a very long, bumpy way in that time. His wife had finally filed for divorce so he was ready to be more forthcoming about the breakup of his marriage.

"You know, Ana and I were together for nine years and we had a great time together for a while," Antonio said in a voice tinted with melancholy. "We went along, side by side, going the same direction for a long time but then something happened—we went in opposite ways. Our lives started to be more separated from one another.

"She wanted to spend more time in Spain and I took the option of working hard on my career in other places and other fields so we didn't get to spend that much time together. At the same time, she didn't really want to come along with me as much as I would have liked. And I understand that because she was trying to make a career in another way."

Others back up Banderas's assertion that he always wanted to include his wife. Ana Nemes, who runs the Keystone Photo Agency in Madrid—and was the first to publish photos of Antonio and Melanie together—says that Banderas was always known to be a devoted husband. And if anyone would know otherwise, it was the Spanish press.

"He always said his wife was his bed of support and that he couldn't do anything without her," Nemes reports. "Ana helped him in everything—he called her his best friend and best fan.

"There were never *any* scandals involving Antonio, he was never known to be a womanizer. He was a family man who was faithful to his wife. Obviously, whatever problems they had, Antonio and Ana kept them very private, which is why so many people were shocked that they were suddenly broken up.

"And understand, Antonio is a very famous person in Spain so people do care. He is a great star, a great native son. While he's no Julio Iglesias," she adds with a bit of a bite, "he is still an important public figure to us."

One of the lesser-known conflicts between Antonio and his wife was her ever-growing interest in Buddhism.

"She really, really got into that," Banderas has said, whose own religious leanings are light at best.

"Ana began spending most of her time at the ashrams and so we saw each other even less. When you stop having intimate time with each other, everything else begins to magnify. Then the more you argue the less physical you are with each other, which in turn causes other insecurities and suddenly, you're hardly talking and seldom touching.

"Sooner or later, with Melanie or without Melanie, it was going to happen. We were destined to go our separate ways. There really was no connection between our breakup and my relationship with Melanie."

Salma Hayek has made this observation:

"I found them to be extremely different from one another. She's a very, very spiritual woman and to be honest, Antonio's not very spiritual. He's into his work and living life and touching what's out there. What he can feel with his hands, taste in his mouth. That's his priority in life."

So while Ana sought comfort in religion, Antonio found solace by falling in love with a costar, the first time he'd ever let himself lose that professional distance.

"I met Melanie right in the middle of my wife turning to Buddhism and me feeling like we had lost each other. I haven't talked to Ana in a while but I am aware she is very angry with me. There were times I wasn't sure she would even grant the divorce, just out of anger.

"For the most part, the lawyers will handle

everything. I want it to be fair and as painless as possible. In Madrid, we have two houses and she will keep one of them. I want to give her as much as she needs to be OK and to be comfortable."

Banderas's sense of remorse is almost visible. He knows that for as much joy as falling in love with Melanie has given him, his happiness has also caused others a fair amount of pain. And complications. Even his work with UNICEF has been put on ice while his private affairs are still being bandied about so publicly.

"I went to Somalia a while back as part of a UNICEF contingent and I had volunteered to go to Sarajevo as well. But they've let me know they want things to settle down a bit before I go anywhere representing UNICEF. And I guess I can understand that. When you are going to do something like that and you want your message heard by your audience, your image has to be completely clean. And now I'm probably not much of an example for society."

But Banderas wanted to make it clear, he has no remorse. Regrets, yes, but no second thoughts.

"Obviously, I loved my wife. We got married and took vows in front of the priest, saying, 'I do.' But life changes, for everybody. I'm not pretending or inventing my feelings. And I don't want to—and should not have to—spend the rest of my life justifying myself."

Nor does it seem he will have to. An interesting

thing has happened since Banderas's emotional return to Spain with Melanie. Suddenly, the crisis appears to be over. His heartfelt pleas fell on listening ears, his sincerity heard and judged to be honest. People are suddenly rooting for him again to be happy.

"Spanish fans were simply bewildered at what was taking place between Antonio and Melanie," explains Ana Nemes. "If Antonio has found the love of his life, then we accept it.

"Nor is anyone shocked at the prospect of divorce. Maybe in the beginning they were but we are more liberal here. If they are in love with each other, if Melanie loves Antonio as much as he loves her, then why would anyone be shocked that Antonio wants to divorce so he can be with Melanie. Everyone has adjusted and gotten used to the fact that they are together and that he's not with Ana anymore."

"In Spain, we don't give a damn who sleeps with anyone," says Katrina Bayonas, Antonio's first Spanish agent. "The Spanish public will love, admire, and envy Antonio Banderas forever. We either want to be him or sleep with him. It's as simple as that."

Like Old Man River, Banderas just keeps rolling along. And the work just keeps coming in. In late 1995, *Four Rooms*, an anthology movie, was released—and was out of theaters a week later. The

ANTONIO BANDERAS

movie was such a small blip on the Hollywood screen, it wasn't even reviewed in most papers. Antonio made a cameo appearance as a favor to pal Robert Rodriguez, who directed one of the four vignettes making up the film.

It's his next project, by far his most ambitious part to date, that is commanding all of Banderas's attention, one that offers him yet another dream-come-true opportunity. It's almost like he's meeting his destiny, playing Che in the long-awaited film version of Andrew Lloyd Webber's *Evita*.

In a funny way, Antonio has come full circle. *Evita* pairs him with his old admirer, Madonna. In fact, Banderas's involvement is directly due to The Material Girl's own influence in casting. As fate would have it, Madonna and Banderas had managed to stay in touch professionally after his *Truth or Dare* appearance and even occasionally ran into each other down in Miami, where Madonna now makes her home.

"I saw her a couple of times and mostly, we just talked about the movie. Then one day Madonna called me and said, 'Antonio, you have to have a meeting with Glenn Gordon Caron,' who was the director originally attached to *Evita*.

"So I did and ended up spending an afternoon at the Disney studio meeting people and recording songs. A while later, the producer called me and said, 'Antonio, we're going to do it and you've got

187

the part.' I couldn't believe it, I was going to get to do a big movie musical.''

But the road to *Evita* hasn't been an easy one—it's taken longer to get to the screen than Evita Péron was even in power. It's a project that has been on and off more than a light switch so it was not all that surprising that shortly after being told he had the part, the project hit a snag. There were budgetary problems and before you could say dictatorship-in-Argentina, the movie was in turnaround, a Hollywood term for limbo, Purgatory—take your pick for what you call oblivion. It eventually took more than another year for the project to be given a green light, but it has finally made it through development hell. This time it really was a go, with Alan Parker attached as director.

The news it was definite was music to Antonio's ears.

''You know, I love musicals.''

So we've heard.

''I remember in 1975 when I didn't have a penny, putting money together to buy the record of *Evita*. I think Madonna will be perfect as Evita. The only thing that worried me was working with the playback. But because Madonna knew all about that from all the videos she's done in her career, I was able to learn from her.

''The singing was no problem. The truth is, I'm really a frustrated rock star. I play piano and guitar and built my own recording studio and I've done that for years as a hobby and now finally, I have the opportunity to use all this music practice professionally. Besides, you know, everybody can sing now. Let's face it, they have machines in the studios now that can put your voice on a track and make you sound great."

In January, Banderas flew to London to join Madonna and the rest of the cast to record the vocals. Griffith tagged along, prompting some friends to point out that she's still just *this much* nervous about Madonna.

"Melanie wasn't going to give Madonna the chance to seduce Antonio," laughs a friend. "She was glued to him in London and joined him on location when he was in South America filming. She saw *Truth or Dare*, too."

Antonio denied that either he or Griffith were worried that Madonna would try to take romantic advantage of him while working together.

"It's not a deep relationship," he has said of Madonna. "I think we'll have a wonderful time together. Professionally. She's sweet and very tough at the same time. She's a girl with problems, a girl with moments of brilliance, sad moments, someone looking for a laugh. When you meet her, she's like a friend that you've had all your life. Madonna and I have become great friends, but no more. And Melanie is secure with that.

"Besides, I survived Madonna once, and I'll survive her twice."

Looking back, Antonio has said it's funny how everything works out for the best, if you only follow your instincts.

"I could have used Madonna back during that time in Spain and it would have been faster for me," Antonio has pointed out. "It would have been perfect for me—I would have gotten immediately all the attention.

"But I said no, because I didn't fall in love with that woman. You see, I don't want anyone to ever say to me, 'Ah, ha! You came here and because of your face or this or that, you got this part.' I can say no, I stared from the bottom and worked my way up like everyone else and it's the truth.

"I prefer it that way—to make a platform and rise from a solid structure than to rise suddenly like, BOOM!"

Besides, even if Madonna did have designs on Banderas, she's too late. He's spoken for. And if there was any doubt about Antonio and Melanie's commitment to one another, it has been put to rest. First, in January 1996, while attending the annual Golden Globe Awards, Melanie and Antonio announced they were expecting a baby. Her third, his first.

"Melanie was dying to get pregnant with Antonio's child from practically the moment she met him," admits a close girlfriend. "But Antonio wanted to wait. He didn't want Melanie to get pregnant before the divorce was taken care of, out of respect for Ana.

"Once that was settled, they went for it. Antonio couldn't be more thrilled."

Banderas has said he always wanted children but the time never seemed right before, he was always too busy. But now ambition may be taking a back seat. After the forced self-reflection of 1995, maybe it's time to slow down, enjoy what he's achieved and take the time to put his private life first for a while.

"He's never really done that before," points out a friend. "Antonio's been so driven to succeed for so long, that he's missed out on some things, like starting a family. But it could be that Melanie caused him to rethink his priorities. He doesn't have to be so obsessive about his career anymore. He's one of the best and doesn't have to go out and prove his talent the way he did when he was young. He's paid his dues."

The news of the baby has caused Banderas's family to come around.

"We get along fantastic," now mama Banderas has said.

"I think she is very attractive," Jose Banderas has offered. "The most important thing is that Antonio is happy. And if Melanie makes him happy, so be it."

In February 1996, Griffith's divorce and

property settlement became final. (She got the Porsche, Planet Hollywood stock, two horses, and a David Hockney painting; Don Johnson got the property in Aspen and Beverly Hills, a 1949 pickup truck, and the jet.)

Finally, on May 14, 1996, during a filming break for *Evita* in London, Antonio and Melanie were quietly married in a fifteen-minute civil ceremony. For all the hoopla surrounding their can't-get-enough-of-you courtship, their legal union was curiously subdued. Ever the professional, friends have suggested that Antonio became concerned that his artistry and acting ability were being overshadowed by the carnival atmosphere surrounding his personal life.

For Banderas, it was time to get serious again. Suddenly he was feeling a pressure familiar to many of his American peers—the need to have a commercially successful film.

Banderas is gratified to hear that his countrymen wish him well. A Madrid news station devoted a segment to asking people on the street their thoughts about Antonio and the answers reflected a benevolent mood.

"I think they are just adorable."

"They seem to be very much in love."

"She's not extremely friendly, but she is enchanting."

"I think everyone should leave them alone and let them love each other."

Banderas couldn't say it better himself.

After *Evita*, before he has a chance to say don't cry for me, Antonio will put his action-adventure face back on—or in this case, mask—playing that swashbuckling hero, Zorro, for Steven Spielberg and company. Not only does *Zorro* give him a chance to be yet another action hero, this one in the Old West, but he gets to ride a horse, too—and play a gallant, noble Spaniard to boot.

"When I do this type of movie, I feel like a kid. It takes me back to my early years playing Indians and cowboys with my brother in Málaga. It's fun—once in a while. But you know, Zorro was a Latin action hero created by Hollywood," Banderas pointed out correctly.

"For many years the Spanish community has not really been represented on film. An action movie like *Desperado* doesn't reflect the Latin community the way films like *My Family* or *The Mambo Kings* do but audiences are grateful to see a character who mirrors themselves.

"That is valuable, because this country is full of so many different races, idioms, accents, and religions—and there is room for everybody onscreen.

"I feel very Spanish and very integrated into the community but at the same time, I feel international, like I am from everywhere. A citizen of the world, you could say. I don't like to make separations between human beings. I prefer to be just myself."

The lack of Spanish characters that audiences can be proud of is a subject that gives Banderas a lot of food for thought. As he grows older, he feels more responsibility to add to the arts and his culture, rather than just enjoying the fruits of his involvement.

"For me, the best of all possible worlds would be to have a bridge between Spain and Hollywood and to work in both countries, back and forth," Banderas has said dreamily.

"I don't want to be bought, by anybody. As an actor, my country is the world. If I receive a script from India, I'll go there. That's the way it is for all actors, I think. It's like a language. When you meet even very big stars—I think of when I worked with Meryl Streep, Jeremy Irons, Tom Hanks, or Tom Cruise—we have the same language. We speak the same idiom. And that's very wonderful, when you find that kind of relationship that transcends the borders."

One of his dreams is to start putting the Spanish classics on film. The first on his list is Zorilla y Moralis's *Don Juan Tenorio*. Natch.

"I've always dreamed of doing the classic version, in Spanish, with a Spanish crew, the whole thing in verse," Antonio has said excitedly. "You know, the British, they've had the opportunity to put Shakespeare, their ancient culture, up there on the screen. Spain never did that but I would like to bite that cake and see if it's possible.

"I've been working as an actor since I was fourteen and now I feel that I need to tell stories from my own point of view. I would like to direct and produce movies in the future, although that is probably something I will have to do in my own country."

Maybe not. At the rate he's going, Antonio will have a free ticket to try anything he wants, at least once. Plus, the studios aren't stupid. They know that the Latin community in America is one of the fastest growing in terms of a consumer group. In Los Angeles, for example, the most widely listened-to radio station happens to be Spanish-speaking. The most watched of any news program is the five o'clock report on KMEX, the Spanish station.

Banderas is a man coming along in the right place at the right time. The world really is his oyster, if he so chooses. For all his modesty, even Antonio realizes he's in an enviable spot.

"Yes, right now I am having a good time in terms of what they call being hot in Hollywood," he has said without ego.

"I feel like I am receiving a bit of reward for twenty years of hard work. But I know that you have to learn to deal with the flops, too. I don't want to lose the capacity for failing or doing something bad. Now people are saying I'm sexy, cool action hero, blah, blah, blah.

"But what happens when I'm in something not

so good? It's going to be, 'Oh, Antonio's losing his power.' You're only as good as the last thing you were in. But I'm used to that. I've done a bunch of movies in my life that were not successful. But I've always worked. First of all, because in Spain you have to do a lot of movies just to survive—movies you like and movies you don't like so much—because you don't make very much money in Spain.

"There, it's an adventure. You make movies with your sweat, your blood, your soul. Here in America, you makes movies with money. I was never looking to be a celebrity, that's an accident. It's an unavoidable result but I try to avoid it as much as possible. I'm not going to criticize the star system, because it's something you can play or not play, but I really don't think I'm that kind of guy.

"The other day, someone was asking me, 'How do you feel now that you're the hottest actor in town.' And if you think about it seriously, one of the hottest actors in town in 1995 was a pig. It's true. *Babe* was a movie that did tons of millions of dollars, so you are in the same package.

"And I don't feel really special to be compared with a pig."

No matter what happens in America, back home he is still and will remain their golden boy—the local kid who did good in the big, bad world. Even if he had to leave home to do it. Even if he never goes back full time.

"I'm like an international soccer star. They feel

proud of me and when I was there, people would stop me on the street and tell me, 'You have to win an Oscar someday.' And I want to—for them as much as for myself.

Although Hollywood seems to be having a passionate love affair with Banderas, he has admitted he was a reluctant lover at first.

"It was not love at first sight. It was more she won my heart little by little. What bothers me the most about Hollywood is that everyone here seems consumed with the business of movie making instead of its artistry. I hate that. I hate it when you go to dinner and all someone at the table talks about is money. It's such . . . bad taste.

"There are so many differences between Spain and America. Probably not as many with New York, which is a more open city, but the lifestyle in Los Angeles is very different. After having spent time in Spain after being away for so long, I can see it more than before.

"The food, the way people talk to each other are different. I mean, in Spain we eat dinner at midnight while in America they're having dinner at seven in the evening. In Spain, everybody smokes. Here, nobody smokes.

"One of the things that really impressed me and surprised me about Los Angeles is that the people don't want to die. They don't even want to look older. They want to look eternally young, clean and wonderful. The skin has to be perfect like velvet and even if they're seventy years old, they feel like they're fifteen. I guess Hollywood is a good place for vampires because the people are trying to buy immortality."

So what's it feel like to have Hollywood at your feet? His old friend Almodovar doesn't think America knows what to do with Antonio, how to best use his talents. But Antonio reportedly doesn't seem bothered by either all the attention—or the fall some seem to be waiting for.

"I don't feel freaked out. I don't feel fear. I've been in this profession twenty years and I believe exactly when they say 'action' and 'cut.' That's where I still want to focus my energy, in that moment. That's what I've looked for my whole life.

"I love acting and I love telling stories but I'm going to slow down, swear. Just to create mystery about your own personality, you have to disappear for a while.

"Until then, I am just trying to live as well as possible in the best way I can. I'm very skeptical in my career and in my life. I prefer to go slow, like riding a horse. My life is full of questions and most of them don't have answers. I'm living the adventure of my life. Now it's here, tomorrow, I don't know. Ultimately, I'm not a master in all of this—I am a student.

"I think that a human being is the most wonderful thing. I just feel very grateful for my life and

I understand very clearly that I am in command of what I do and the decisions that I make."

Banderas stubbed out his last cigarette and hunched back in his chair, assuming a classic European pose. He looked off in the distance and when he looked back, Antonio was smiling with familiar self-knowledge. For as much as life goes on and changes, some things remain comfortable the same.

"But I'm like any other actor." He flashed a charming smile. "I just don't want to grow up."

He was a charming hitchhiker with a body to die for in *Thelma and Louise*. He was the sensuous undead in *Interview with the Vampire*. And in *Legends of the Fall*, his first big romantic lead, he was simply drop-dead gorgeous. How did a sensitive Missouri boy end up as the male sex symbol of the 1990s?

It's time to get a closer look at the real Brad Pitt— an irresistible mix of hellraiser and choir boy who dropped out of college just two credits short of graduating to head for Hollywood.

Packed with lots of details, and 16 irresistible pages of photos, Chris Nickson's stunning biography is the best way to get into Brad Pitt's world.

Go behind the scenes into the life and career of Hollywood's sexiest hunk

BRAD PITT

CHRIS NICKSON